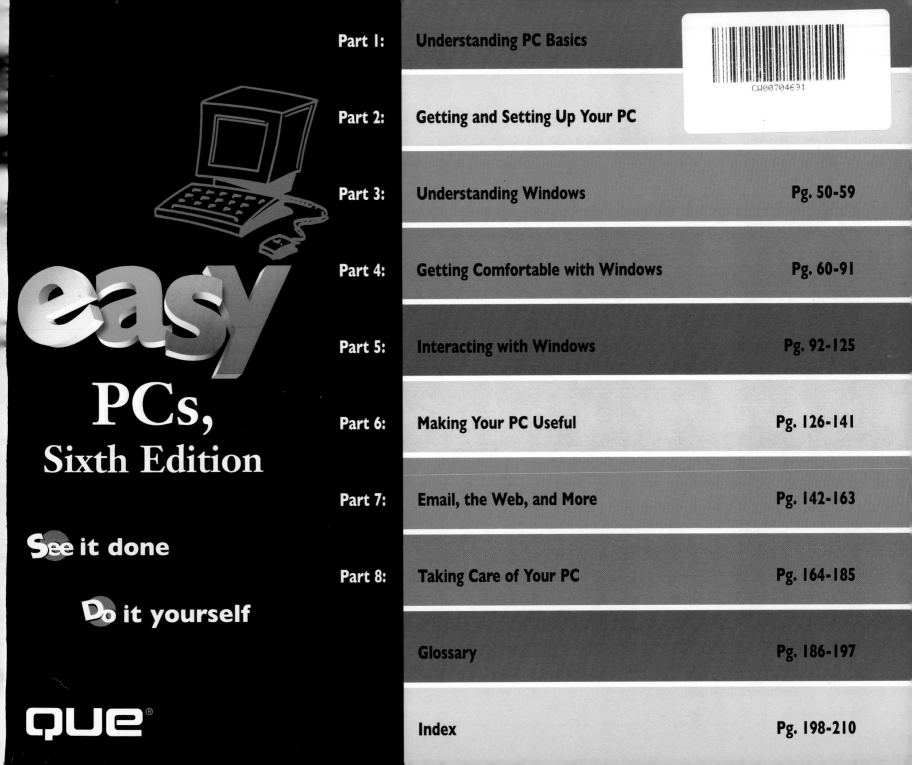

easy PCs, Sixth Edition

See it done

Do it yourself

que®

CW00704691

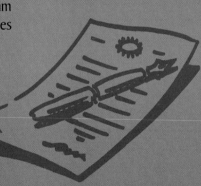

Part 6: Making Your PC Useful

Part 7: Email, the Web, and More

Part 8: Taking Care of Your PC

Copyright©1999 by Que® Corporation

Library of Congress Catalog No.: 99-62407

ISBN: 0-7897-2104-x

00 99   6 5 4 3 2 1

Interpretation of the printing code: The rightmost double-digit number is the year of the book's printing; the rightmost single-digit number, the number of the book's printing. For example, a printing code of 99-1 shows that the first printing of the book occurred in 1999.

Executive Editor
Christopher Will

Development Editor
Kate Welsh

Technical Editor
Kyle Bryant

Managing Editor
Thomas F. Hayes

Project Editor
Linda Seifert

Indexers
Sandra Henselmeier
Christine Nelsen

Book Designers
Gary Adair
Anne Jones

Cover Designer
Anne Jones

Illustrations
Laura Robbins

Production Designers
Lisa England
Trina Wurst

Proofreader
Jeanne Clark

How to Use This Book

It's as Easy as 1-2-3

Each part of this book is made up of a series of short, instructional lessons, designed to help you understand basic information that you need to get the most out of your computer hardware and software.

① Each step is fully illustrated to show you how it looks onscreen.

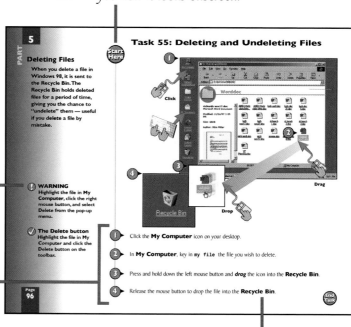

Click: Click the left mouse button once.

Double-click: Click the left mouse button twice in rapid succession.

② Tips and **!** Warnings give you a heads-up for any extra information you may need while working through the task.

Right-click: Click the right mouse button once.

② Each task includes a series of quick, easy steps designed to guide you through the procedure.

Pointer Arrow: Highlights an item on the screen you need to point to or focus on in the step or task.

③ Items you select or click in menus, dialog boxes, tabs, and windows are shown in **Bold**. Words in ***Bold italic*** are defined in the glossary. Information you type is in a `special font`.

Selection: Highlights the area onscreen discussed in the step or task.

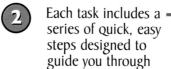

Drag

Drop

Click & Type: Click once where indicated and begin typing to enter your text or data.

How to Drag: Point to the starting place or object. Hold down the mouse button (right or left per instructions), move the mouse to the new location, then release the button.

Next Step: If you see this symbol, it means the task you're working on continues on the next page.

End Task: Task is complete.

Introduction

Hello, and welcome to *Easy PCs, Sixth Edition*! This book will help you use and understand your personal computer. It's the only book you need to get up to speed with your PC.

If you're planning on buying your first PC, *Easy PCs, Sixth Edition* will help you understand what you're buying. You'll learn to tell the difference between hardware and software, between gigabytes and megahertz, and between a bargain and a clunker.

If you already have a PC, *Easy PCs, Sixth Edition* will show you what the various parts are, how they work, and how to take care of them. You'll be guided through setting up your computer and getting it working. You'll also learn to use Windows to run programs and to manage information stored in your PC.

The book is divided into eight parts:

- Part 1, "Understanding PC Basics," teaches you about the parts of your computer, what they do, and how they work. You'll also learn the meaning behind many of the technical terms used in articles on PCs.

- Part 2, "Getting and Setting Up Your PC," helps you with buying a computer and getting it running.

- Part 3, "Understanding Windows," is your guide to how the computer runs programs and organizes your files.

- Part 4, "Getting Comfortable with Windows," and Part 5, "Interacting with Windows," teach you to start and control programs and to organize your files.

- Part 6, "Making Your PC Useful," shows you the different types of programs that are available and what they can do for you.

- Part 7, "Email, the Web, and More," tells you about going online, using modems, the Internet, and the World Wide Web.

- Part 8, "Taking Care of Your PC," teaches you how to keep your PC in good working order and what to do when something goes wrong.

Understanding PC Basics

A computer is a very powerful device, made up of a number of parts with special functions. When you understand what these parts are, what they do, and how they do it, you have an easier time buying and using your PC.

If you've seen articles about PCs, ads for PCs, or other PC books, you've probably encountered a lot of strange terms. Don't worry about it. You can easily learn everything you need to buy and use a PC, and this book helps you do just that. In this part of the book, you aren't inundated with technical terms, but you learn enough of them to understand what those ads and articles are talking about.

Tasks

Task 1: Understanding What a PC Is

Start Here

Personal Computing

Computers used to be huge machines the size of several rooms that aided engineers and even bigger machines that aided mad scientists of the movies. Over the past 20 years, however, they've become handy little boxes that everyone from school children to senior citizens uses.

1 A **computer** is an information machine. It takes information in, works with it, and puts information out.

2 A **personal computer** is a small computer meant to be used by one person at a time.

(3) The terms **PC** and **IBM compatible** have come to mean a style of personal computer based on the 1981 computer made by IBM. Macintoshes and other non-IBM style computers aren't PCs.

(4) PCs are now vital tools for working, playing, and communicating. By using different computer programs, one PC can turn into a thousand different tools.

PC Types and Their Uses

Although all PCs are designed to run the same software, they are made in a number of special ways for particular users and uses.

Task 2: Recognizing PC Types

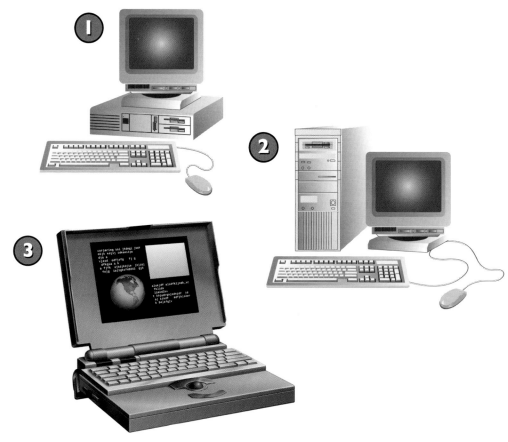

1 The most common type of older PC is the **desktop PC**.

2 Most new PCs are **tower PCs**, which stand upright, so they take up little floor or desk space.

3 **Laptop PCs** (also called notebook PCs) are one-piece computers small enough to fit in a briefcase and designed to run on batteries. They're a great tool for people on the go.

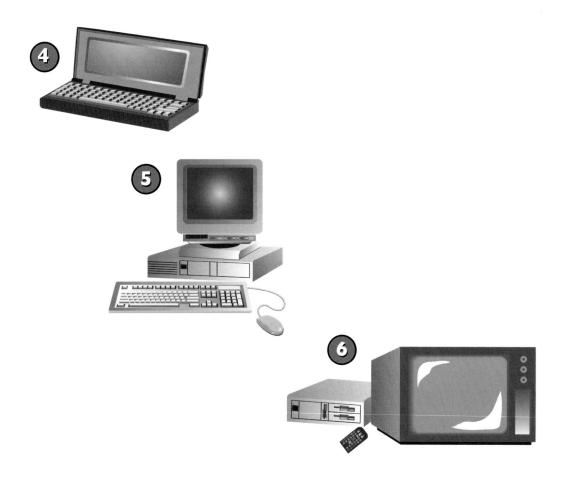

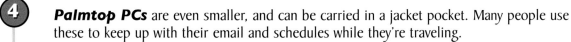

Palmtop PCs are even smaller, and can be carried in a jacket pocket. Many people use these to keep up with their email and schedules while they're traveling.

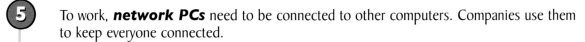

To work, **network PCs** need to be connected to other computers. Companies use them to keep everyone connected.

Home users can buy **entertainment PCs**, which also work as TVs and can be integrated with stereo systems.

Hardware Versus Software

The elements that make up a working computer are hardware and software. *Hardware* is the physical computer—the monitor, system unit, speakers, and so on. *Software* is instructions that tell your computer what to do. Either element alone is useless.

✓ A noncomputer example
A TV is a piece of hardware, and a TV show is like a piece of software. TVs would be useless without shows, and TV shows would be useless without TVs. The video tape on which you save the TV show is a piece of storage media.

Task 3: Understanding Hardware and Software

Start Here

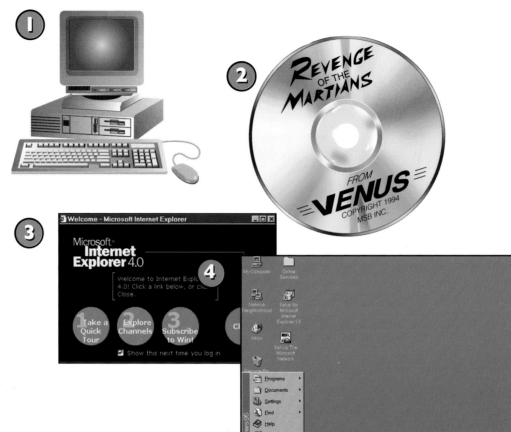

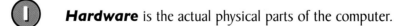

Hardware is the actual physical parts of the computer.

Software is instructions the computer uses. Software is stored on media, such as a CD.

Software includes **programs**; for example, a word processor, a Web browser, or a video game program. A program is a series of commands that enables the computer to do something.

Software also includes **operating systems**—stored information that your computer needs in order to operate.

End Task

Task 4: Understanding Computer Processes

Start Here

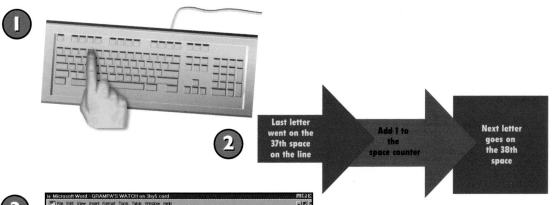

① ②

Last letter went on the 37th space on the line → Add 1 to the space counter → Next letter goes on the 38th space

③

W Microsoft Word - GRAMPA'S WATCH on 3by5 card

File Edit View Insert Format Tools Table Window Help

Body Text   Utah Condensed   9.5   B I U

> My recent search for a watch with a usable light brings to mind my grandfather, who purchased one of the first illuminated watches when they were made available in the 1930's. He had to mail order it from Switzerland. When it arrived, it was a big, thick thing. The light was uneven and dim, but it served its purpose.

Page 1   Sec 1   1/1   At 1.7"   Ln 9   Col 27

④

GRAMPA'S WATCH

How Computers Work

A computer is capable of a wide range of very complex processes, although all computer processes revolve around four very simple elements—*input*, processing, *output*, and *storage*.

① Information that is put into a computer, such as the characters that you type when writing a letter, is called ***input***.

② The word processing program processes the input by performing calculations on it to do the job the program was meant to do.

③ The program then puts out information by displaying the letter on the computer screen. Information being put out is called ***output***.

④ The program also saves a copy of the story so that it can read it later. Keeping information is called ***storage***.

End Task

Task 5: Naming the Parts of Your PC

The Big Pieces

Most PCs are made up of a few standard pieces, connected by cables. Each piece has its own special function. Because PCs are just connected by cables, it's easy to replace any one piece (such as replacing an old keyboard with a new one) without replacing the entire PC.

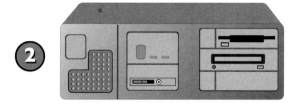

1. The **monitor** is a TV-type screen, which the PC uses to output information to you. (It's also called a **screen** or a **CRT**.)

2. The **system unit** is where all the processing goes on. It also contains your **internal storage devices**.

3. The **keyboard** is an **input device**. You use it to type information into the PC.

4. When you drag the **mouse**, that motion is input. Clicking the mouse buttons is another way to provide input.

5   Most PCs have **speakers**, which are used for sound output, such as beeps or music.

6   A **printer** prints output onto paper.

7   Laptops have the monitor, system unit, and keyboard all built into one piece, making the computer more portable (and more difficult to repair).

Task 6: Looking at the System Unit

The Heart of the Computer

All your PC's real work is done inside the system unit. The processing goes on there, and so does the storage.

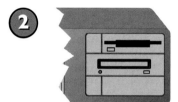

✓ **Look inside your system unit**

The cover is usually held down by a screw in the top center of the back or is hinged without anything holding it closed. Unplug the system and then lift or tilt the cover up by the sides (the front of the unit isn't attached to it).

1 The front of the system unit has the on switch and a reset switch, which restarts the computer without turning it off.

2 The front of the system unit also has the slots and drawers where you insert **removable storage devices** such as CD-ROMs and floppy disks.

3 The rear of the system unit has connectors to connect the system unit to all the other parts of the PC.

Next Step

Front

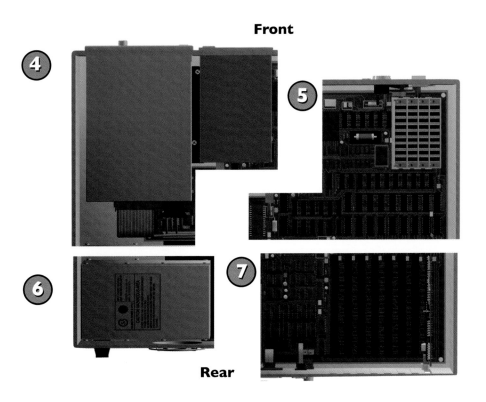

Rear

(4) Inside, you find the storage devices that you saw the front of in step 2, plus the **hard disk**, a nonremovable storage device.

(5) The **motherboard** holds and connects the PC's electronic pieces, including the central processing unit (**CPU**) and the random access memory (**RAM**), a storage device.

(6) The **power supply** converts electricity from a wall outlet to the precise amounts that the parts of the system unit need.

(7) **Expansion cards** add functions to your PC and handle communications with certain input and output devices, such as the speakers and the monitor.

The Brains of the PC

The *central processing unit* (*CPU* for short and also called the *processor*) is a computer chip that does all the processing for the computer. This small chip contains millions of tiny electrical switches (called transistors) that are connected so that they perform calculations.

Task 7: Understanding What the CPU Does

Start Here

GET NUMBER FROM RAM
MULTIPLY IT BY 3
PUT RESULT INTO RAM

WHAT'S THE NUMBER?

2 TIMES 3 IS 6

STORE THE NUMBER "6"

1. The CPU gets the program from a storage device and follows the series of commands.

2. The CPU requests and receives data from input and storage devices.

3. It can calculate and compare numbers.

4. The CPU sends information to storage and output devices.

End Task

Task 8: Understanding CPU Types: Pentium and Others

Start Here

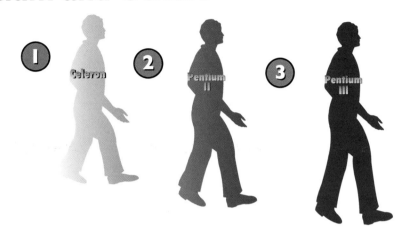

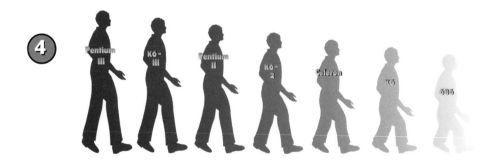

Different Models of CPU

Intel, the company that makes most of the CPUs (central processing units) for PCs, comes out with a whole new model every year or so. The new model is always better because it can get more done in each *cycle*, which is the term used for a single tick of the computer's internal metronome.

1. The **Celeron** CPU (central processing unit) was designed to be cheaper than other processors.

2. **Pentium II** CPUs can do more with each step.

3. **Pentium III** CPUs do even more.

4. Other companies also make PC CPUs.

What are MMX and 3D?

MMX on the end of a CPU's name stands for *multimedia extensions*. MMX chips have added circuitry that enables them to handle audio and video even faster. The *3D* at the end of a CPU's name is similar, indicating it can handle some types of graphics data faster.

End Task

The Rhythm of the CPU

Every **CPU** has a clock, an electronic metronome that sets the speed at which it operates. Every time the clock ticks, the **CPU** performs another step. The clock's speed is measured in *megahertz (MHz)*. The higher the **CPU's** megahertz rate, the faster it runs. Modern **CPUs** run anywhere from 300 to 500 megahertz. If you want your PC to run faster, you may be able to replace your **CPU** with one that runs at a higher **MHz** rate. Check your PC's user manual to find the **CPU** speed limit of your motherboard.

✓ **CPU speed isn't PC speed**
If you get a CPU that's twice as fast, it doesn't make your whole PC twice as fast. The CPU speed only changes how fast processing takes place. Input, output, and storage have their own speeds.

Task 9: Understanding Megahertz and CPU Speed

Start Here

1. In the time that a 300MHz CPU does two steps...

2. ...a 450MHz does three steps.

3. How quickly the CPU gets work done is a combination of the CPU speed and how advanced the CPU is.

4. A less advanced CPU running at a high MHz rate can sometimes be faster than a more advanced CPU with a lower MHz rate.

End Task

Task 10: Understanding the Motherboard

Start Here

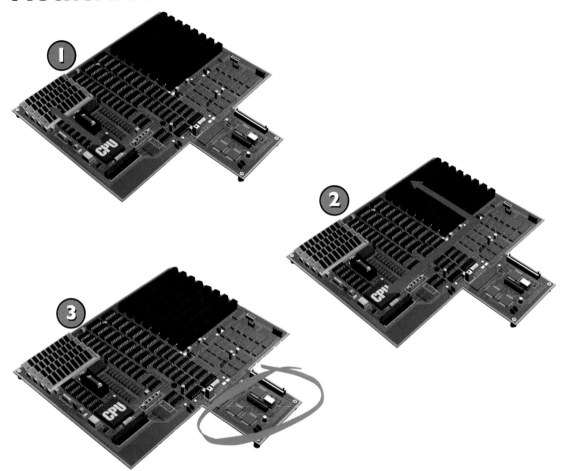

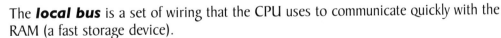

Your PC's Nervous System

Your brain needs the body's system of nerves to receive input from your senses and to output commands to your muscles. The *motherboard* is like the nervous system, enabling all the devices to communicate with the CPU (central processing unit) while making sure that commands from the CPU go to the right place.

✓ **Motherboards with more CPUs**

These days, some motherboards have space for more than one CPU. That way, the PC can get work done more quickly. Windows, however, does not know how to use more than one CPU, so a PC with more than one CPU won't run Windows any faster.

(1) The **local bus** is a set of wiring that the CPU uses to communicate quickly with the RAM (a fast storage device).

(2) The **system bus** is a slower set of wiring the CPU uses to communicate with the other storage devices and most input and output devices.

(3) The **disk controller** is a set of chips that translates the CPU's request for information from storage into commands that the disk drives understand.

End Task

How Much Information Does Your PC Handle?

Your PC has a lot of devices that store or handle information, and they all have limits on how much information they can handle. New words have been invented to describe quantities of information.

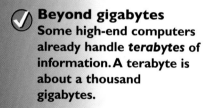

✓ **Beyond gigabytes**
Some high-end computers already handle *terabytes* of information. A terabyte is about a thousand gigabytes.

✓ **Why is a kilobyte about 1000 bytes?**
A kilobyte is actually 1024 bytes. A megabyte is actually 1024 times 1024 bytes, and so on. 1024 is an easier number for the PC to handle than 1000.

Task 11: Measuring Data

Start
Here

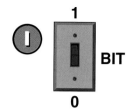

1

I **BIT**

0

2

BYTE

③ B = 66

1 The smallest amount of information is a *bit*. A bit can hold only one of two values: 0 or 1.

2 Eight bits strung together make a *byte*. There are 256 combinations of 1s and 0s possible, used to represent the numbers 0 through 255.

3 The PC uses a code called *ASCII* to store letters and punctuation as numbers, giving each character a different value.

Next
Step

(4) B

BYTE

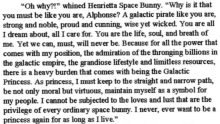
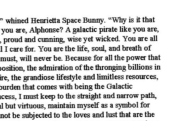
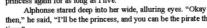

(5)

"Oh why?!" whined Henrietta Space Bunny. "Why is it that you must be like you are, Alphonse? A galactic pirate like you are, strong and noble, proud and cunning, wise yet wicked. You are all I dream about, all I care for. You are the life, soul, and breath of me. Yet we can, must, will never be. Because for all the power that comes with my position, the admiration of the thronging billions in the galactic empire, the grandiose lifestyle and limitless resources, there is a heavy burden that comes with being the Galactic Princess. As princess, I must keep to the straight and narrow path, be not only moral but virtuous, maintain myself as a symbol for my people. I cannot be subjected to the loves and lust that are the privilege of every ordinary space bunny. I never, ever want to be a princess again for as long as I live."

Alphonse stared deep into her wide, alluring eyes. "Okay then," he said, "I'll be the princess, and you can be the pirate this time."

"Cool!" she said, twitching her ears and smiling a broad grin.

KILOBYTE

(6)

MEGABYTE

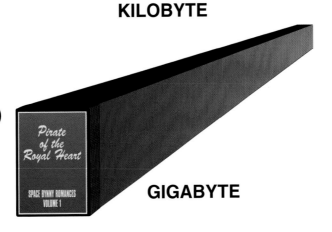

(7)

GIGABYTE

(4) One byte can hold one letter.

(5) One **kilobyte** (abbreviated **KB** or just **K**) is about 1000 bytes, and holds about a half page of text.

(6) One **megabyte** (abbreviated **MB** or **meg**) is about a million bytes, and holds about as much text as a nice, thick novel.

(7) One **gigabyte** (abbreviated **GB** or **gig**) is about a billion bytes, and can hold about a thousand novels.

Task 12: Using RAM and ROM

Memory

The computer has two types of memory storage chips: *RAM* (random access memory) and ROM (read-only memory). These memory chips are connected to the motherboard, and aren't removed except when fixing or improving your PC.

✓ **How much RAM?**
Most modern PCs have between 8 and 64 megabytes of RAM.

✓ **RAM speed**
Some PCs still use *regular RAM* (also known as *DRAM*, dynamic RAM). Some use the faster *EDO RAM* (extended data output RAM), and some use the even faster *SDRAM* (synchronous dynamic RAM).

Start Here

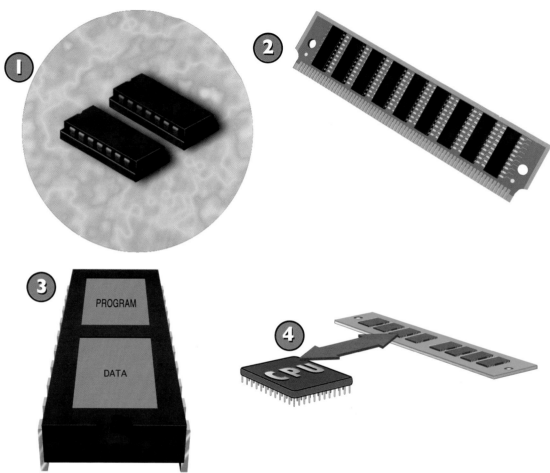

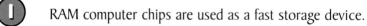

(1) RAM computer chips are used as a fast storage device.

(2) RAM chips come on **SIMMs** or on **DIMMs**—two types of memory-holding add-in cards. These cards plug into the motherboard.

(3) Your PC stores programs and data with which it is currently working in RAM.

(4) RAM is good for short-term storage, because the CPU gets information from it quickly. RAM loses its data when the PC is turned off, so it can't be used for long-term storage.

Next Step

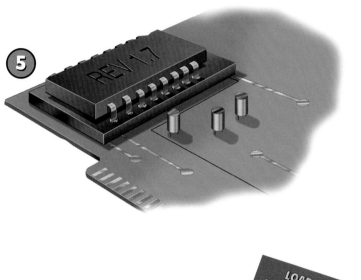

5 ROM stands for read-only memory, which means the PC can get data from it, but can't change or add to it. ROM keeps the data that it holds even when the PC is turned off.

6 The ROM holds the boot program. The boot program helps the CPU find the hard disk where Windows is stored, so that Windows can be loaded.

ROM stands for read-only memory, which means the PC can get data from it, but can't change or add to it. ROM keeps the data that it holds even when the PC is turned off.

The ROM holds the boot program. The boot program helps the CPU find the hard disk where Windows is stored, so that Windows can be loaded.

Task 13: Using Your Hard Disk

Start Here

Long-term Storage

The *hard disk* (sometimes called the C drive) is your PC's main storage device. It holds your software files all the time, whether your CPU currently needs them or not.

✓ **Hard drives store gigabytes**
Most modern hard drives hold from 1 to 10 gigabytes.

✓ **PC slowing down?**
If your PC has been slowing down, your hard disk may be too full. If you use up more than 90% of your hard disk's space, either get rid of unneeded files or have an additional hard disk installed in your PC.

✓ **Take it easy on the hard disk!**
The hard disk is a delicate mechanism. Don't move your PC while it's running, and never try to open the hard disk's case. Doing either ruins your hard disk.

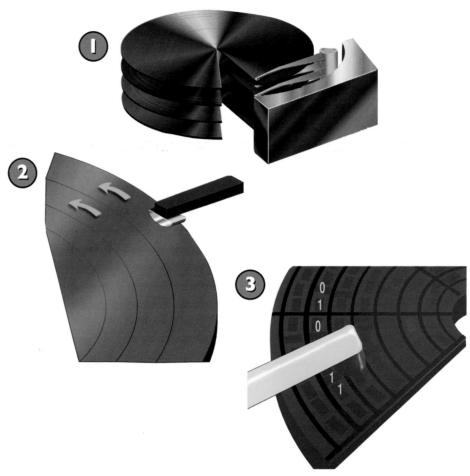

(1) The hard disk is a pile of spinning platters, locked permanently in a metal case inside your system unit.

(2) The disk-reading head moves over each platter like a record player needle moves over a record.

(3) Data is stored magnetically on your hard disk, much the same way audio or video tape recorders store sound and images on tape.

End Task

Task 14: Using CD-ROMs and DVDs

Start Here

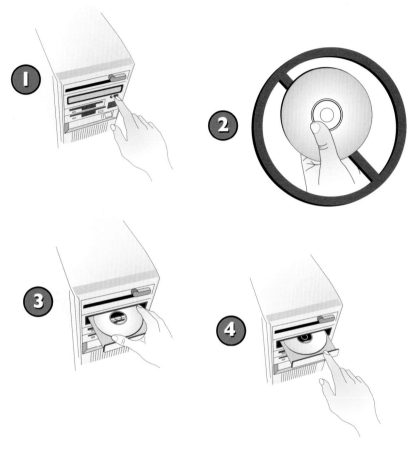

Large Amounts of Software

A *CD-ROM* (compact disc–read-only memory) is a removable storage device that holds up to 600 megabytes and can be read by any **CD-ROM** drive or **DVD** drive. A *DVD* (digital versatile disc) holds close to 5 gigabytes, and can be read only by **DVD** drives. Because they are read-only, your **PC** cannot add or change data on **CD-ROM** or **DVD** discs. Because these discs can hold so much data, complex programs usually come on **CD-ROMs** or **DVDs**.

 CD-ROM drive speed
Speed measurements are based on how quickly an audio **CD** player reads data. Most current **CD-ROM** drives range from 4x (4 times the speed of a CD player, or about 600 kilobytes per second) to 32x, but 12x is about as fast as you're likely to need.

① Push the button on the drive to open the tray and remove any disc that's already in there.

② Hold the disc by the edges, never by the flat sides. Fingerprints on the disc can make it unreadable.

③ Put your disc, printed side up, into the circular indent on the drive tray.

④ Push the front edge of the tray lightly, and the drive closes.

End Task

Task 15: Using Your Floppy Disk

Another Removable Storage Device

Like the **CD-ROM**, a *floppy disk* (often just called a *floppy*) is a removable storage device. Although floppy disks hold much less data than a **CD-ROM**, they are useful for storing spare copies of data from your hard disk. Floppies are cheap, and almost every **PC** can read and write to them.

✓ **Get formatted disks**
Most disks are sold already *formatted* (set up to hold the data for a particular type of computer). Make sure the disk box says they're Windows, IBM, or PC formatted.

✓ **Write-proofing your floppy**
The little plastic switch on the bottom side of the disk, near the edge away from the metal shutter, is the *write-protect switch*. Push it open, and the disk drive won't be able to write to or erase the disk.

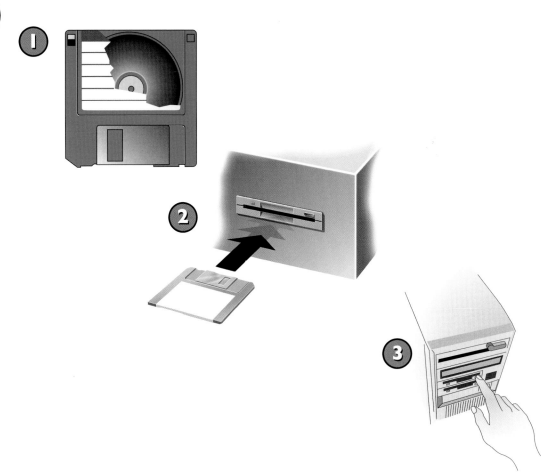

① The floppy disk is a circle of magnetic material stored in a plastic case.

② To read or write to a floppy disk, push the floppy disk into the *floppy drive* slot.

③ Push the button on the floppy drive, and the disk springs out.

Next Step ►

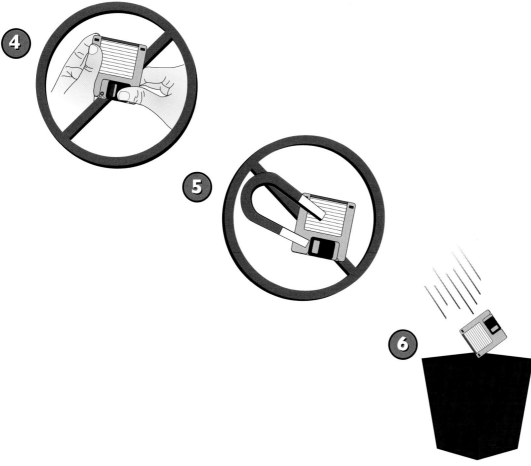

(4) Don't slide open the metal shutter on the disk. You can contaminate the disk with dust and smears.

(5) Keep the disk away from magnets and devices that create magnetic fields, including anything with a large motor.

(6) If your PC has trouble reading a floppy, it alerts you. Throw the floppy away; it could have dirt on it that could hurt your floppy drive.

End Task

Transporting a Lot of Data

The floppy disk is the main medium for copying files from your computer for use elsewhere. Unfortunately, the floppy disk only holds about 1.5 megabytes, so if you wanted to copy all the files on your hard disk, you'd need about a thousand of them. A number of other devices have been invented to enable you to copy large amounts of information from your machine.

Task 16: Understanding Larger Removable Storage Devices

Start Here

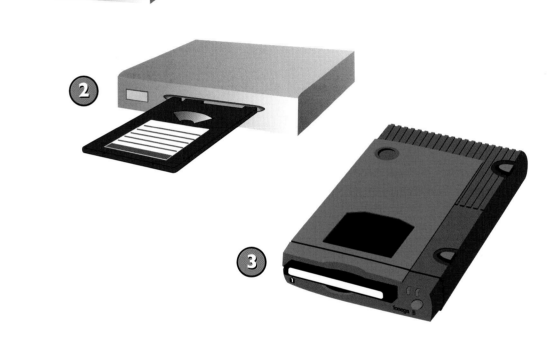

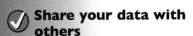
Share your data with others
The best large-storage drive for sharing data with others is the CD-R (compact disc–recordable) drive, because almost everyone has a CD-ROM drive that reads the discs.

① **Tape drives** store hundreds of megabytes or even gigabytes on each tape cartridge, which costs from $5 to $50. They're used to store backup copies of hard disk files.

② **LS-120 SuperDisk** and **zip drives** read and write special $15 floppies that store around 100 megabytes. Zip drives are popular for transporting large art files.

③ **Jaz drives** are the most popular brand of **removable hard disks**. The 1-gigabyte disks cost $100 each, and are removable like floppies but fast like a hard disk.

Next Step

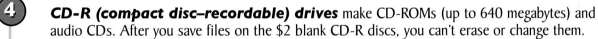

CD-R (compact disc–recordable) drives make CD-ROMs (up to 640 megabytes) and audio CDs. After you save files on the $2 blank CD-R discs, you can't erase or change them.

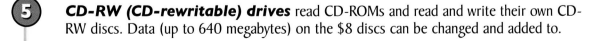

CD-RW (CD-rewritable) drives read CD-ROMs and read and write their own CD-RW discs. Data (up to 640 megabytes) on the $8 discs can be changed and added to.

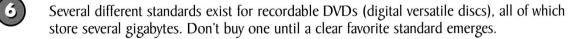

Several different standards exist for recordable DVDs (digital versatile discs), all of which store several gigabytes. Don't buy one until a clear favorite standard emerges.

Task 17: Using Expansion Cards

Adding Features to Your PC

Inside your system unit are *expansion slots*—places to install *expansion cards*, computer boards that add functions to your computer. Most expansion cards handle communications to devices outside the system unit; for example, you have a *video card*, which sends the picture to your monitor; a *sound card*, which sends sound to your speakers; and probably a *modem*, which communicates with other computers over the telephone line.

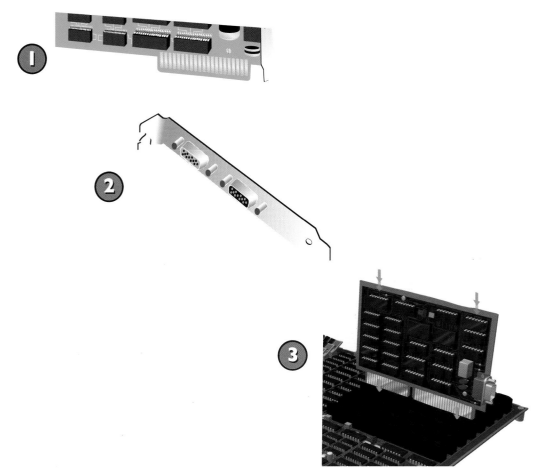

① The **backplate** of the expansion board fits into a slot on the back of the computer. Connectors on the backplate can be used to connect outside devices to the card.

② The connectors on the bottom edge of the card are for communication with the motherboard and to get power from power lines in the PC.

③ **ISA (industry standard architecture)** cards plug into ISA expansion slots, which communicate with the CPU over the system bus (see Task 10).

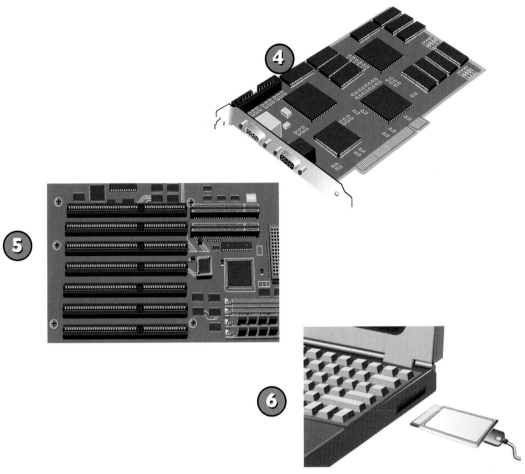

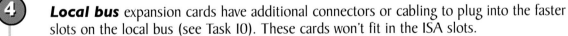

(4) **Local bus** expansion cards have additional connectors or cabling to plug into the faster slots on the local bus (see Task 10). These cards won't fit in the ISA slots.

(5) Three types of local bus cards are available with different connectors: VLB, PCI, and AGP. Before you buy an expansion card, check your PC's documentation to see what kinds of cards it has slots for.

(6) Laptops don't have room for normal expansion cards, but some have special slots that take **PC Cards** (also known as **PCMCIA** or **CardBus cards**).

Printing to Paper

A printer prints your documents onto paper. Modern printers can print not only on standard paper but also on envelopes, stickers, business cards, party invitations, transparency sheets, and even T-shirt iron-ons!

 Start Here

Task 18: Using Your Printer

(1) Print instructions:
- "Nat likes Lara" at top in blue
- 5 inch circle in lower right corner
- This image in circle:

(2)

Comics Sans MS
Courier New
Arial
Times New Roman

(3) Nat likes Lara

(1) Your PC describes the page to the printer, sending some things as digitized graphics, some as shapes, and some just as text.

(2) The PC also describes the **font** (type style) to the printer, so the printer can use that font design on the text.

(3) A processor inside the printer converts the font information into a grid of dots that makes up each letter. The more dots per inch that a printer prints (its **resolution**), the better the page looks.

 Next Step

Nat likes Lara

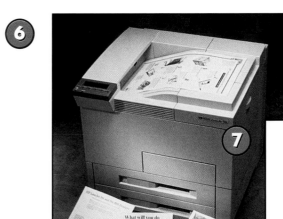

Nat likes Lara

4 An **inkjet printer** prints the page by squirting dots of ink onto the paper.

5 Inkjet printers can print in color. Color ink can be expensive, and you can use it up quickly by printing photographs.

6 A **laser printer** has a cylinder that uses static electricity to pick up **toner**, which it presses onto the paper.

7 Except for very expensive models, laser printers print only in black and white. Laser printers make sharper-looking printouts than inkjets do.

End Task

Task 19: Handling Sound and Pictures

Multimedia

Most modern PCs are designed for multimedia (quality sound and graphics). A good multimedia PC includes a good video adapter (an expansion card or portion of the motherboard that sets up the screen image) and a sound adapter (like a video adapter, except that this handles the sound for the speakers). You can improve your sound and video by buying newer, better adapters.

Start Here

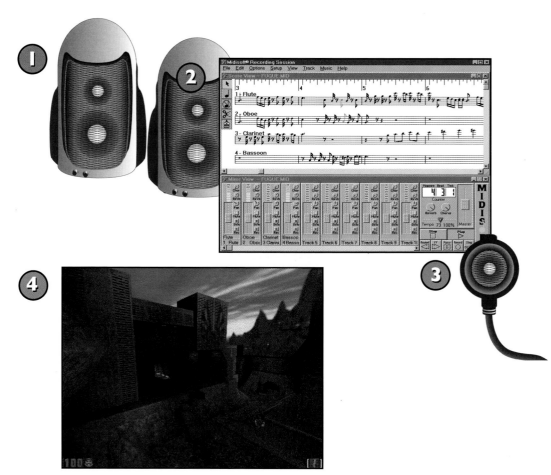

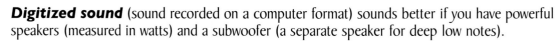

✓ **Movies on your PC**
If you're buying a DVD (digital versatile disc) drive so that you can watch DVD movies on your PC, you need to get a video adapter with **MPEG** (Moving Pictures Expert Group) video capability.

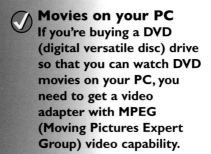

1 *Digitized sound* (sound recorded on a computer format) sounds better if you have powerful speakers (measured in watts) and a subwoofer (a separate speaker for deep low notes).

2 MIDI (musical instrument digital interface) music is stored as a series of notes, similar to sheet music. A sound adapter with a wavetable (recorded instrument sounds) makes this sound better.

3 Adding a good microphone to your PC enables you to record sound, and to use voice dictation software, so you can speak into your word processor instead of typing.

4 A video adapter with 3D capability enables you to play games set in amazing 3D worlds.

End Task

Task 20: Scanning Pictures

Start Here

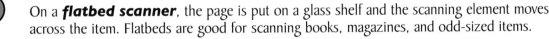

Using a Scanner

A *scanner* is a device that takes a digital picture of a page, a photograph, or a drawing and sends it to your PC. After you have the image on your PC, you can change it, print it out, or use it in your documents.

✅ **Scanner resolution**
This is measured in *dots per inch (dpi)*. More dpi means better resolution.

✅ **What is interpolation?**
Interpolation is a system where a program estimates what color each dot would hold if the scanner were scanning at a higher resolution. When shopping for a scanner, ignore the interpolated resolution (usually 4800–9660 dpi); the optical resolution (300–1200 dpi) tells you how good the scanner really is.

1 On a *flatbed scanner*, the page is put on a glass shelf and the scanning element moves across the item. Flatbeds are good for scanning books, magazines, and odd-sized items.

2 Paper gets pulled through a *sheetfed scanner* in the same way that it gets pulled through a fax machine sending a fax. Sheetfed scanners are good for scanning big stacks of pages.

3 You can use a scanner to scan in photos to add to your documents.

4 **OCR (*Optical Character Recognition*)** software can take the text from a scanned page and put it into your word processor.

End Task

PART 2

Getting and Setting Up Your PC

A PC is a major purchase. It's not cheap (although it can be an excellent deal), and it's something that you could end up spending more time with than you do with your car or your pet. (If you spend more time with it than you do with your spouse, it's time to take a vacation!)

In this part, you get some tips on where you can purchase PCs, places to look for good deals, and pitfalls to watch out for. You also learn how to assemble the pieces of your PC. This may seem like a daunting task, but it really is easy if you take it a step at a time.

Tasks

Task 1: Shopping for Your PC

Start Here

Where to Buy?

It seems that you can buy PCs on almost any block, whether it's at a department store, an electronics store, or at a place that specializes in computers. You can order PCs from magazine ads, from catalogs, and over the World Wide Web. Each outlet has its strengths and its weaknesses. Because PC prices often go down quickly, you can't spend a long time looking around, or you're comparing today's prices against last month's.

- 7GB Hard Disk
- 32MB EDO RAM
- 233MHz PII
- Software bundle

✓ **Get the latest price**
When mail-ordering a PC, check the prices in the latest magazine ad and compare them to the prices on the company's Web site. Tell them where you saw the lowest price, and you can probably get that price.

① Department and appliance stores can have good prices on standard packages that you can take home today, but some try to sell slow-moving older models at "bargain" prices.

② A local PC shop builds your PC to order using common components. This is great if you have special needs and can wait a few days, but some shops are slow to respond to problems.

③ Many respected PC manufacturers sell mainly through magazine ads and Web sites. They can customize your PC somewhat. Many offer hardware repair service in your home.

④ To run next year's software, make sure your PC has at least a 300MHz processor, a 7-gigabyte hard disk, 64 megabytes of RAM, 3D graphics, and a CD-ROM drive.

Next Step

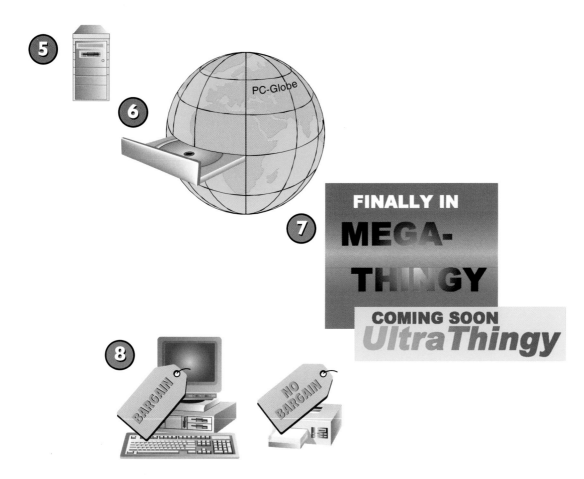

(5) Some cheap PCs don't have additional **drive bays**, the spaces on the PC's front where you add a tape drive, a DVD drive, or something else you want to add.

(6) Beware of strangely shaped or slim-line computers. They may be hard to repair or upgrade later.

(7) Computer manufacturers always tout some super new feature coming to PCs in a few months. If you always wait for the new feature, you never get around to buying the PC.

(8) Don't automatically buy the printer where you buy the PC. Better prices can often be found elsewhere. (Some appliance stores shine when it comes to printer prices.)

 Used PCs
A used PC can be cheap, but remember that someone had a reason to get rid of it. It may work fine, but it's probably not the latest design and will likely be outdated soon.

 End Task

Task 2: Reading a PC Ad

Listing the Pieces

Most printed PC ads these days show a list of components that make up each model (computer components are discussed in detail in Part 1 of this book). These lists may look like a barrage of technospeak, but useful information can easily be gleaned from them, if you know what to look for.

Start Here

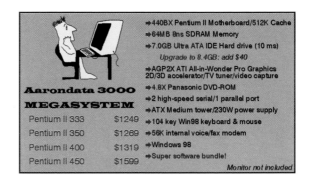

Aarondata 3000 MEGASYSTEM

Pentium II 333	$1249
Pentium II 350	$1269
Pentium II 400	$1319
Pentium II 450	$1599

→440BX Pentium II Motherboard/512K Cache
→64MB 8ns SDRAM Memory
→7.0GB Ultra ATA IDE Hard drive (10 ms)
  Upgrade to 8.4GB: add $40
→AGP2X ATI All-in-Wonder Pro Graphics 2D/3D accelerator/TV tuner/video capture
→4.8X Panasonic DVD-ROM
→2 high-speed serial/1 parallel port
→ATX Medium tower/230W power supply
→104 key Win98 keyboard & mouse
→56K internal voice/fax modem
→Windows 98
→Super software bundle!

Monitor not included

1
→440BX Pentium II Motherboard/512K Cache
→64MB 8ns SDRAM Memory
→7.0GB Ultra ATA IDE Hard drive (10 ms)
  Upgrade to 8.4GB: add $40

2
→AGP2X ATI All-in-Wonder Pro Graphics 2D/3D accelerator/TV tuner/video capture
→4.8X Panasonic DVD-ROM

3
→7.0GB Ultra ATA IDE Hard drive (10 ms)
  Upgrade to 8.4GB: add $40

4
→Super software bundle!

✓ Can't find the right model?
If the ad doesn't list the exact components that you need, ask for the combination that you want. Most PC stores and mail-order houses make custom PCs.

✓ Avoid stores without Windows
If a PC store doesn't offer Microsoft Windows, they're likely either too small an operation to trust or they've been caught installing bootlegged Windows on PCs.

1 The speed and capacity of components are listed (these ratings are explained in Part 1 of this book). Higher numbers are better, except things marked ***ns (nanoseconds)*** or ***ms (milliseconds)***.

2 Brand names are a good sign. Otherwise, they're probably fobbing off whatever brand is cheapest at the moment.

3 You can't have too much hard disk space. If they offer a larger hard disk for a little more money, take it.

4 Programs in the software bundle are usually listed. The bundle is useful unless you want specific programs.

Next Step

5  ➡Windows 98

6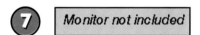

Pentium II 333	$1249
Pentium II 350	$1269
Pentium II 400	$1319
Pentium II 450	$1599

7 *Monitor not included*

8

5 You need Windows, so make sure that it's included. If not, the store will probably charge you $100 extra for it. (Don't be fooled by "Windows keyboard" in the ad; that's just a keyboard.)

6 Most ads give you a choice of different processors and speeds. The best bargain is often the second-fastest one. The added speed of the fastest is usually not worth the added cost.

7 Frequently, the monitor isn't included in the price. This enables you to pick your own monitor (they vary widely in size and quality; bigger is better) or use a monitor from an older PC.

8 Check for components that aren't listed. This ad lists everything you should expect a system to have except a sound card and speakers. If it isn't listed, it's probably not included.

What's a voice/fax modem?
A *modem* enables your PC to talk to other computers over a phone line. A modem with voice/fax capability enables you to use your PC as an answering machine or fax. (You learn more about modems in Part 7.)

End Task

Task 3: Finding a Good Place for Your PC

Where to Set Up

When you get your new PC home, don't just set it up in the first place you can find. If you take some time to find the right place, you can make your PC easier to hook up and use.

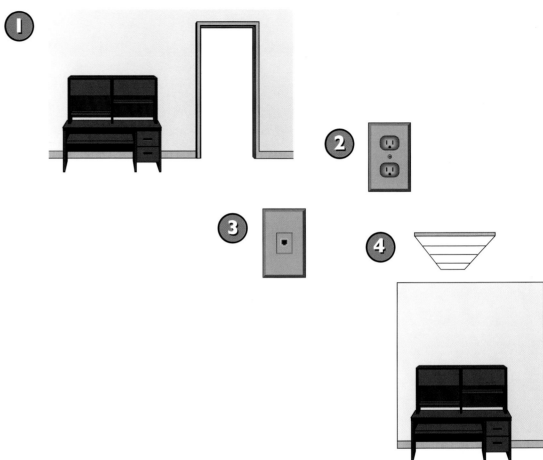

Start Here

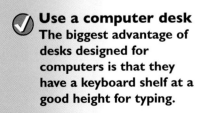

✓ Use a computer desk
The biggest advantage of desks designed for computers is that they have a keyboard shelf at a good height for typing.

① The desk or table that you put your PC on should be sturdy, stable, and away from where people may run into it. (Bumping a PC while it's running can ruin the hard disk.)

② It should be near at least two three-pronged electric sockets. These sockets should be on a different circuit from your dishwasher, refrigerator, clothes washer, and dryer.

③ If you're going to use a modem, you need a nearby phone jack.

④ The desk should be well lit. A light directly overhead is best so that you don't see the lightbulb's reflection in the monitor.

End Task

Task 4: Setting Up the Pieces of Your PC

The Big Pieces

In Part 1 you learned the names of all the main components of a computer. The first step to putting your PC together is to put the main pieces where they belong. It's easier to put everything in place and then cable everything together than to try to cable each piece and then slide it into place so that everything doesn't get tangled.

⚠ WARNING

Don't plug anything in yet. Plugging in the power cords is the last step in assembling your PC; plugging it in sooner could damage components.

✓ Subwoofer goes under the desk

The subwoofer that comes with better PC speaker systems goes under the desk. Put it far back, to keep from accidentally kicking it.

1 Desktop system units belong on the desk. Tower system units taller than 14 inches go on a static-protection mat on the floor. Leave at least 6 inches behind the PC for cables.

2 The monitor goes on top of a desktop system unit. If you're using a tower, use a monitor stand or other sturdy base to bring the monitor up to eye-level when you're sitting.

3 Speakers go to the left and right of the desktop system unit. For a tower PC, put them to the left and right of the monitor. If one speaker has controls on it, it goes on the right side.

4 The printer can go off to the side and out of the way. It can even be put on its own table.

Task 5: Connecting Your Keyboard

The Keyboard

While you're connecting your PC, you may not want to put the keyboard right where you'll be using it. If you put the keyboard off to the side, you may be able to slide your PC forward a few inches, which makes it easier to get to the back of the PC to connect every-thing. (It's safe to slowly slide your PC on the desk when it's turned off, but don't do that while it's on.)

WARNING
Don't just stick the connector into the hole and twist it until it fits. You could bend or break the pins.

Help with lining up
Most keyboard cables have an alignment indicator—a flat edge or a raised line on the connector plug that matches a similar line on the case surrounding the connector socket. The pins are lined up when the flat edge is on the top or bottom or when the indicator lines are aligned.

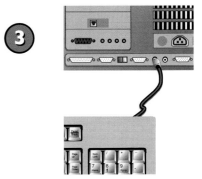

1 The semicircle of pins in the plug on the keyboard cable...

2 ...needs to line up with the semicircle of holes in the round socket on the back of the PC.

3 Press the connector gently but firmly into place.

Task 6: Connecting Your Mouse

Start Here

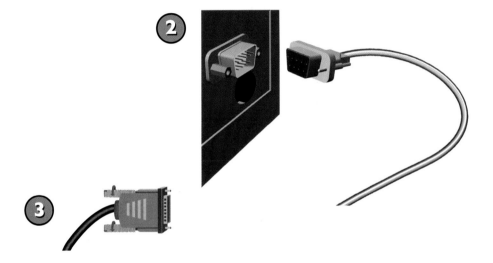

The Mouse

Your mouse should end up to the right of your keyboard if you are right-handed, and to the left of your keyboard if you are left-handed.

✓ Which 9-pin connector?

Your PC may have two 9-pin connectors built in. If one has a number 1 or a picture of a mouse next to it, pick that. Otherwise, use the upper connector.

✓ Female and male connectors

Computer documentation often refers to a connector with holes in it as a *female connector* and one with pins in it as a *male connector*.

1 The connector with 9 holes at the end of your mouse cable...

2 ...plugs into a 9-pin connector built into the back of your PC. (Do not plug it into any 9-pin connectors on the edge of the expansion cards!)

3 Use your fingers to screw the bolts on the sides of the mouse cable end into the nuts on the PC. This keeps the cable from coming loose.

End Task

Task 7: Connecting Your Monitor

The Monitor

You attach the monitor to the output of the video adapter, a set of chips that processes the display information. On most systems, these chips are on an expansion card. On some systems, they are built into the motherboard. In either case, you can upgrade your system with an expansion card when a better video adapter is available.

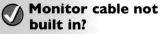 **Monitor cable not built in?**
Most monitors have a built-in cable. If your monitor doesn't, you have to attach the cable at both ends.

 The D-shaped connector with 9 pins at the end of your monitor cable...

 ...plugs into the D-shaped connector with 9 holes on the back of your PC. (This connector socket is often marked with a monitor symbol or the word Monitor.)

 Use your fingers to screw the fasteners on the sides of the monitor cable end into the sockets on the video card. This keeps the cable from coming loose.

Task 8: Connecting Your Sound System

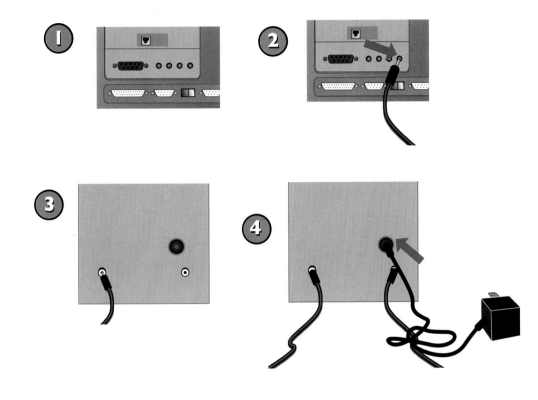

The Speakers

You attach your speakers either to the *sound card* (an expansion card that manages the PC's sound information) or to sockets built into the back of your PC (if the motherboard has sound chips). If your PC speakers came with an AC/DC power plug adapter, they are *amplified speakers*. If they didn't come with a power plug adapter, they are *unamplified speakers*, which have poorer-quality sound.

① WARNING
Do not hook to your PC speakers that aren't designed for computers. They emit magnetic radiation, which can harm parts of your computer.

✓ Connecting a microphone
The microphone connects to the Mic In plug on the sound card.

① On the back of the PC you can see several similar-looking jacks, each marked to show what it's for.

② If you have amplified speakers, plug the speaker cable into the hole marked Line Out. If you have unamplified speakers, plug the cable into the hole marked Speaker.

③ If the other end of the cable isn't built into a speaker, plug it into the speaker that has the jack. (You may also have to plug the other speakers into that speaker.)

④ If these are amplified speakers, plug the power adapter into the speaker.

Task 9: Connecting Your Modem

Hooking Up to the Phone Line

A *modem* is a device that enables your PC to communicate with other computers via a telephone line. Most new PCs come with *internal modems*, modems that are expansion cards inside the PCs. The connectors for these modems are on the modem's backplate, the edge of which is visible on the back of your PC.

✓ **Wrong type of phone jack?**
If your phone jacks are different from the jacks on the modem, you need a jack adapter, available at any electronics store.

✓ **Extra steps for external modems**
Connect the modem cable from the 25-hole connector on the external modem to a 9-pin connector next to the mouse connector on the PC. Then attach the power adapter to the modem.

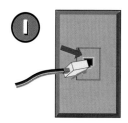

1 Plug one end of the phone extension cord (which comes with your PC or modem) into the phone socket in the wall.

2 Plug the other end of the phone extension cord into the socket marked Line or Telco on the modem's backplate.

3 If you want a phone near your computer (and you don't care whether it shares a phone line with the modem), plug the cord from the phone into the jack marked Phone on the modem's backplate.

Task 10: Connecting Your Printer

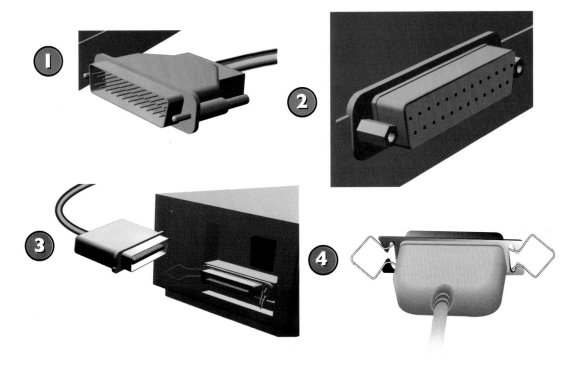

The Printer

A number of steps are involved in setting up your printer that are specific to your printer model. For example, you have to put paper in the paper bin and possibly install an ink or toner cartridge. That information is in your printer manual.

1 Plug the end of the 25-pin printer cable...

2 ...into the 25-hole connector on the back of the PC, and use the fasteners on the sides of the connector to tighten the connection.

3 Plug the other end of the cable into the matching connector on the printer.

4 Squeeze the diamond-shape wires next to the printer's connectors in toward the connector to lock the connection in place.

Task 11: Connecting Your Power Cords

The Surge Protector

Some of the electronics in your PC are quite delicate, needing an even flow of electricity. Unfortunately, the power coming from your electrical socket can sometimes have a *surge* (an increase in power level). To prevent a surge from burning out parts of your PC, it's wise to use a *surge protector*. But beware of cheap models—a good surge protector costs $20 to $40.

✓ **Blackouts and lightning can kill PCs**
Unplug your surge protector and your modem phone line during lightning storms and blackouts, and plug them back in after the storm is gone and the lights are restored.

⚠ **WARNING**
Although you can plug lights into the surge protector, don't use it to plug in motorized appliances such as air conditioners. They can cause additional surges.

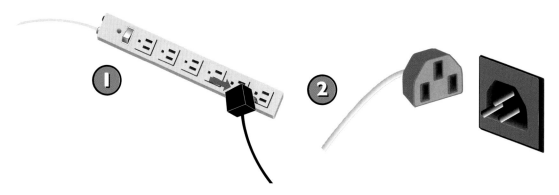

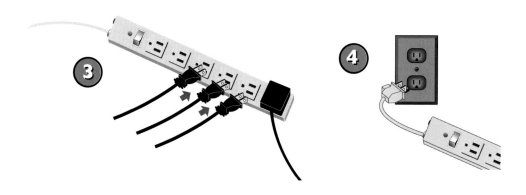

(1) Plug the speakers' power adapter into the last plug of the surge protector.

(2) Plug the smaller end of the PC's power cord into the back of your PC.

(3) Plug the power cords of the PC, the printer, and the monitor into the surge protector.

(4) Plug the surge protector into the wall socket.

Task 12: Turning On Your PC

Start Here

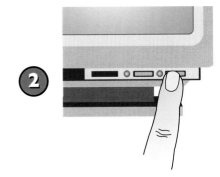

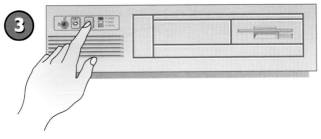

First, turn on the power switch on the surge protector.

Next, press the power button on the monitor.

Finally, press the power switch on the front of your PC.

Powering Up

Turning on your PC is quite easy. Turning off your computer is quite easy, too, but you should not try that until you've read Part 4, Task 8, which explains the method for turning off your PC without accidentally damaging the information stored on your hard disk.

✓ Save energy

Many new PCs and monitors are Energy Saver designed. This type of system does not have to be turned on and off each time you use it. Instead, when you're done for the day, you can put the system into a shutdown or sleep mode in which it uses very little energy. In this mode, the system will usually have a light blinking on the front to let you know it is still plugged in and on. To start it back up, just press the "on" switch on the front.

End Task

Understanding Windows

Windows is your PC's operating system, the software that controls all the other software on your PC, making sure that they all can use and share the screen, the disks, the printer, and the other parts of your system. Windows also sets up how you interact with the programs, making sure that all programs have a similar interface so that they are easy to use.

In this part of the book, you learn more about the different kinds of Windows and what they can do for you. You learn how Windows organizes all the information on the disk, so you can store and retrieve information easily.

Tasks

Windows Is an Operating System

An *operating system (OS)* is a computer's main program. The OS is in charge of understanding the commands that you give to start programs. It's also in charge of maintaining the information stored on your disks. Other programs pass the information to be stored on the disks to the OS and ask the OS for information needed from the hard disk. Windows is the operating system on almost all PCs sold today.

✓ **Versions of Windows**
At the time of this writing, Windows 98 is the standard version of Windows. It's a slight update of Windows 95. Other Windows versions that you may see include the older Windows 3.11, Windows for Workgroups, and the more powerful Windows NT.

Task 1: Understanding the Windows Operating System

System Requirements

To run SPACE BUNNY SQUADRON, you need:

- •Processor: **Pentium or better, running at 200MHz or faster**
- •Hard Disk: **50 MB available space**
- •CD-ROM drive: **4x or faster**
- •Joystick
- •**Windows 95 or above**

 Programs are designed to work with specific operating systems. Before you buy a program, check the box to make sure that it's designed for your Windows version and your PC.

 Windows has a standard format for the way program controls look and work; after you learn to control one program, you know a lot about controlling all programs.

 These controls and the program's work area are displayed in a *window* in which you do all your work. In Part 4 of this book, you learn to change the size and position of windows.

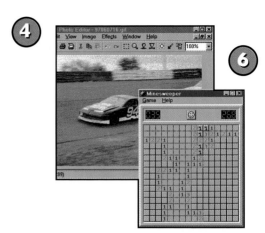

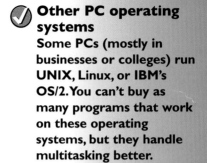

Other PC operating systems
Some PCs (mostly in businesses or colleges) run UNIX, Linux, or IBM's OS/2. You can't buy as many programs that work on these operating systems, but they handle multitasking better.

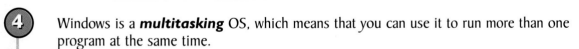

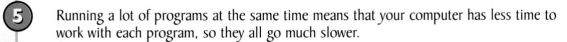

(4) Windows is a *multitasking* OS, which means that you can use it to run more than one program at the same time.

(5) Running a lot of programs at the same time means that your computer has less time to work with each program, so they all go much slower.

(6) Windows comes with several programs, including games, a calculator, and an art program.

End Task

Your View of Windows

The screen that Windows displays has a variety of elements, each with a different function. Against the background (called the desktop), you see small pictures (icons), a small arrow (the pointer), and a gray bar (the taskbar) that runs along the bottom of the screen and contains the Start button. You also see rectangular program display (windows).

Task 2: Recognizing the Parts of the Windows Screen

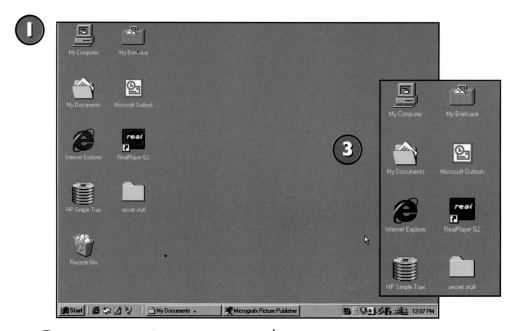

① The background that fills your screen is the **desktop** (yours may be a different color or design). All the tools that you need to work with in Windows programs are on the desktop.

② The **taskbar**, which holds the Start button, is on the bottom of the screen. The taskbar also holds icons for any open programs. (You learn how to use the taskbar in Part 4.)

③ **Icons** are little pictures on the Windows desktop that represent a program, a command, or a **file** (a set of stored information). Each icon is labeled with its name.

④ The **pointer** is an arrow you use to select things onscreen. You move the pointer with the mouse. (A colorful pointer is used in this book because it's easy to see.)

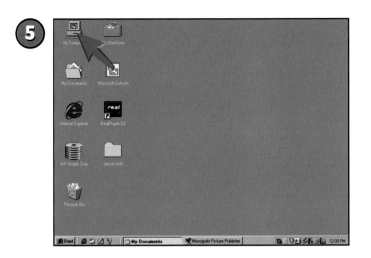

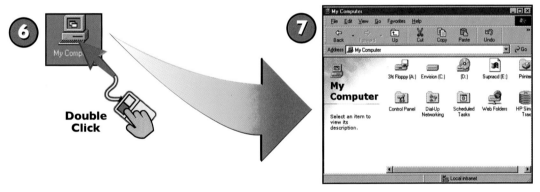

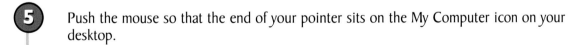

Double Click

5. Push the mouse so that the end of your pointer sits on the My Computer icon on your desktop.

6. With the pointer on the icon, press the left button on your mouse twice, quickly. (This is called *double-clicking*, and is used to start the program or function the icon represents.)

7. A *window* opens. This window shows icons that represent some of the devices in or connected to your computer.

End Task

Task 3: Knowing Your Drive Names

Every Drive Has a Name

Your computer uses drives (such as the hard drive, the floppy drive, and the CD-ROM drive) to organize and store programs, data, and other information. Windows labels each drive with a letter and a colon and uses this label to indicate on which drive information is stored. You can see the icons for these drives in the **My Computer** window that you opened in the previous task.

✓ **Disk or drive?**
You may hear the hard drive referred to as a *hard disk*. Don't be confused—these terms are used interchangeably.

✓ **Where's B:?**
Many older PCs had two floppy drives. The second floppy drive was B:.

(1) When you open your My Computer window (see Part 3, Task 2), you see icons, which represent the drives on your computer.

(2) You always have one *floppy drive* named A:. This is where you insert *floppy disks*—removable information storage disks. (To learn more about floppy disks and drives, see Part 1, Task 15.)

(3) You have a *hard drive* named C:. This is your computer's nonremovable disk, in which programs and data are stored. (For more on hard drives, see Part 1, Task 13.)

(4) Your CD-ROM drive is probably D:, but it may be another letter. Use this drive to load software, play music CDs, and more. (CD-ROM drives are discussed in Part 1, Task 14.)

Task 4: Understanding Files

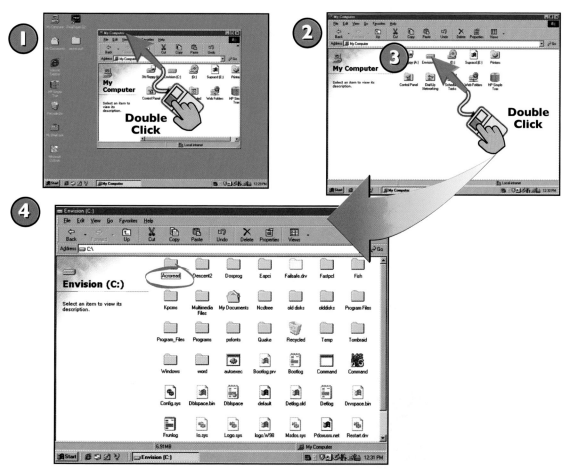

1 Double Click

2

3 Double Click

4 Envision (C:)

All Information Is in Files

The information on the hard drive is organized into *files*. A file is made up of a complete group of information. For example, one file, named calc.exe, holds the complete calculator program. A file can also be a letter, spreadsheet, or other document. When you create a file, you can give it a name that makes it easy for you to find and identify in the future.

✅ The hidden filename extension

Each filename ends with an *extension*, a period and three letters that indicate for the PC the format of the file's information. For example, files with .TXT on the end hold text, whereas filenames with .PIC hold pictures. Windows usually (but not always) hides the extension when showing filenames.

1 With the My Computer window open (as explained in Part 3, Task 2), double-click the words My Computer in the **title bar** at the top of the window.

2 The My Computer window should now fill the whole screen. (If it doesn't, repeat step 1.)

3 Double-click the **C:** drive icon.

4 The window now shows icons for some of the files on the C: drive. The name at the bottom of each icon is the filename.

End Task

Task 5: Understanding Folders

Folders Contain Files

Your hard drive has literally thousands of files on it. If they were all kept on one list, it would be hard to find a specific file. To make it easier to manage all those files, they are organized into *folders*, files that hold other files inside them. If you think of a hard disk as a big filing cabinet that holds all your files, you might have one folder with all your bills and another with all your letters.

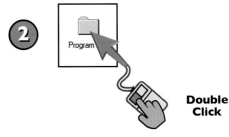
Double Click

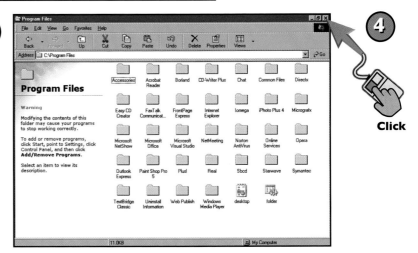
Click

In the window displaying the contents of the C: hard disk (as explained in Part 3, Task 4), you see some file icons that look like manila folders. These files are *folders*.

Double-click the **Program Files** folder.

Now you see the contents of the **Program Files** folder. As you can see, a folder can hold other folders inside it.

Click the **Close** button (the **X** button in the upper-right corner of the window) to close the window.

Task 6: Naming the File Path

Start Here

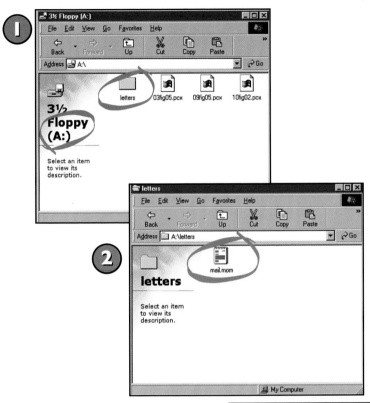

Every File Has a Precise Location

Sometimes programs and documentation need to refer to the exact location of a file. To do this, they list the disk name, followed by the names of all the folders that you have to go through to find the file, and ending with the filename. Each name is separated from the next using a \ character (called a *backslash*).

A:\letters\mail.mom

1. If the disk in your floppy drive (your A: drive) contains a folder named **letters**...

2. ...and in that folder you have a file named **mail.mom**...

3. ...then the full file path for that file is **A:\letters\mail.mom**.

End Task

Getting Comfortable with Windows

Windows is the one piece of software on your machine that you most need to understand. Because it's your operating system, it's running all the time, even when you're running other programs. After you learn to use the Windows user interface, you'll know most of what you need to run most other programs.

This part won't turn you into a Windows master, but it should get you going. If you're using Windows 98, then you may want to learn more by reading ***Easy Windows 98***.

Tasks

Starting Windows

Most PCs sold these days
come with Windows
already installed. If
Windows is not installed on
your PC, get someone with
a bit of experience to help
you install it. Installation is
not difficult, but it does
involve some decisions with
which an experienced user
can help.

Task 1: Starting Windows

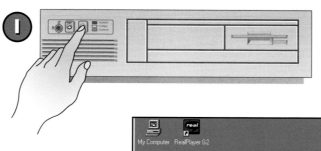

1 Turn on your computer.

2 The computer spends time loading the Windows program and making sure that your computer is properly working. During loading, the pointer looks like an hourglass.

3 When the pointer is just an arrow and the **taskbar** is visible, you're ready to go!

✓ **Did DOS start up?**
If your computer starts up
in DOS, just type windows
and then press the Enter
key.

Task 2: Recognizing the Parts of a Window

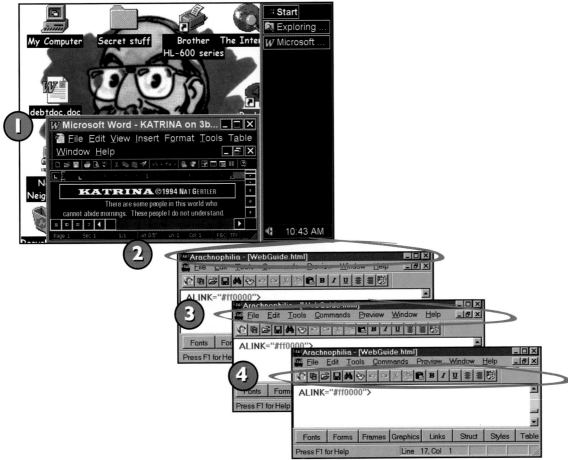

The Window

Programs display information in *windows*, which are rectangles on the screen that include menus and other controls. The windows appear in front of the background, which is called the *desktop*.

① The window is the rectangular area on the screen.

② The *title bar* at the top of the window usually has the program name and often has the name of the document displayed in the window.

③ Immediately under the title bar of most windows is the *menu bar*, with a list of command categories.

④ Many windows have *toolbars*, rows of buttons for giving commands. Usually these are near the top or the bottom of the window.

✅ Windows looks different?

I've customized the colors and lettering on the first screen that you see on this page so that you can see how different Windows can be made to look. If Windows looks different on your PC, don't worry; it still works the same.

Mouse Pointer

The *mouse* is the main device you use to give the computer commands and to *select* and move things onscreen (when you need to enter typed information, use the keyboard).

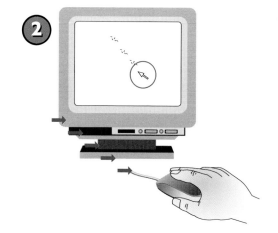

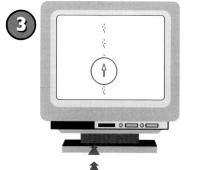

✓ Trackballs

Trackballs work much the same as a mouse, except that you drag your hand across the mouse, rather than drag the mouse across the table.

1 Put your hand on top of the mouse. The forward edge of the mouse (the edge with the buttons) should point straight ahead.

2 Drag the mouse sideways across the mouse pad. The pointer moves in the same direction.

3 Pushing the mouse moves the pointer up the screen. Pulling brings it down.

4 To *point* to something on the screen, you have to put the end of the arrow on it, not just aim toward it.

Task 4: Dragging with the Mouse

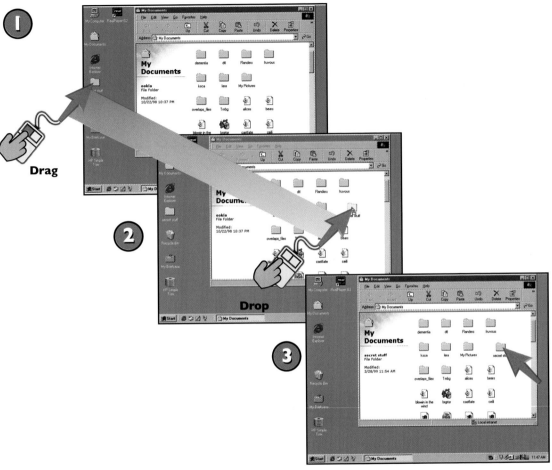

Drag

Drop

Dragging

Dragging is a way of using the mouse to move an object from one position to the other on the screen. It's also used to tell the computer on which area of the screen you want it to work, such as what text you want to copy.

1 Point to an icon. Push down the left mouse button and hold it down.

2 With the button pushed down, slide the mouse. A copy of the icon's shape follows the pointer. This is *dragging*.

3 Release the mouse button. You've now *dropped* the icon.

 Left-handed?
If you're left-handed, you can set up your mouse for easier use (see Part 5, Task 29).

Clicking

Clicking is a mouse action used to indicate a specific item or location onscreen.

Task 5: Clicking

Click

Double Click

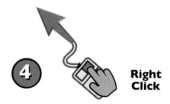
Right Click

✔ **Choosing buttons**
When this book says to *choose* a button, choose it by clicking it.

✔ **Click less**
If you're using Windows 98, some of the things that this book tells you to double-click only need one click. (Double-clicks still work fine.)

① To *click* something, you have to point to it first.

② *Click* what you're pointing to by quickly pressing and releasing the left mouse button.

③ *Double-click* what you're pointing to by clicking twice in rapid succession.

④ *Right-click* what you're pointing to by quickly pressing and releasing the right mouse button.

End Task

Task 6: Starting Programs from the Start Menu

Start Here

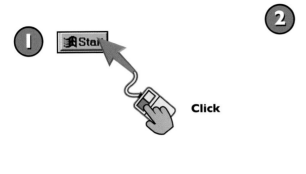

Click

Click

Opening the Start Menu

Windows enables you to start any program quickly with just a few moves and clicks of the mouse. The Start button is your shortcut to starting anything.

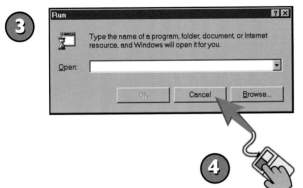

Click

1. Click **Start**.

2. On the menu that appears, click **Run**.

3. You've successfully started the Run program!

4. Click **Cancel** to stop the program.

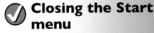

Closing the Start menu
To close the Start menu without choosing anything from it, click **Start** again or click any blank area outside the Start menu.

End Task

Task 7: Using a Start Submenu

Start Submenus

Only a few commands end up on the main Start menu. Most end up in one of the submenus—menus you can bring up by selecting an item on the Start menu.

Click

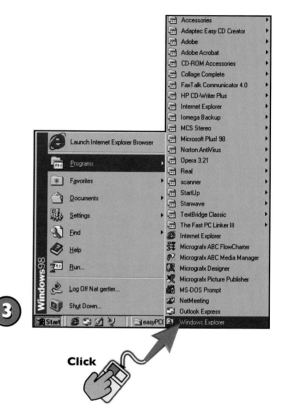

Click

 Choose **Start**.

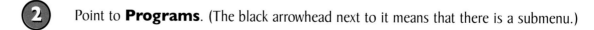 Point to **Programs**. (The black arrowhead next to it means that there is a submenu.)

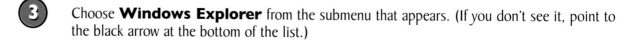 Choose **Windows Explorer** from the submenu that appears. (If you don't see it, point to the black arrow at the bottom of the list.)

Next Step

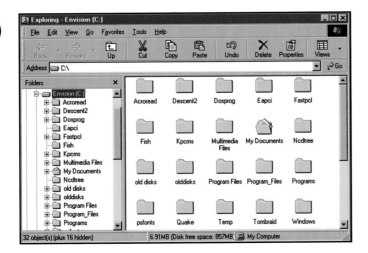

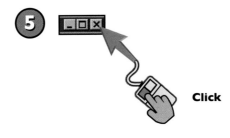

Click

4 The Windows Explorer program starts!

5 Choose the **X** button to close the Windows Explorer program.

✅ **What's on the submenu?**
Most programs are in the Programs submenu.

✅ **Nested submenus**
Many submenus have other submenus within them.

End Task

Task 8: Turning Off the Computer

Shutting Down Windows

You should never just turn off your computer. Instead, you have to give Windows a command that tells it to stop doing everything, and wait until it finishes before turning it off.

Start Here

Click

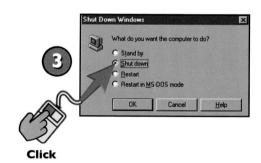

Click

Click

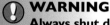

① Click **Start**.

② From the Start menu, choose **Shut Down**.

③ Click the option button next to **Shut down**.

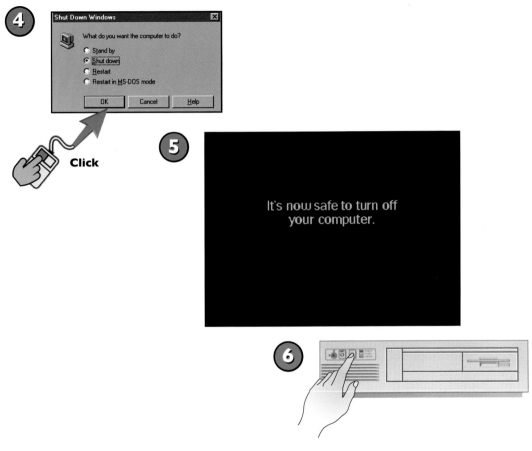

Click

It's now safe to turn off
your computer.

(4) Choose **OK**. (If you don't have an OK button, choose **Yes**.) If your screen goes totally blank, it means your PC is in low-power shutdown mode. You're done!

(5) If this screen appears, your PC doesn't have shutdown mode.

(6) Now you can turn off the computer and monitor.

Task 9: Opening and Closing a Window

Opening and Closing

When you give the command to start most programs, the program opens one or more windows. These windows are your means of communicating with the program. When you are finished with the information in the window, you can *close* it to free up space on your screen.

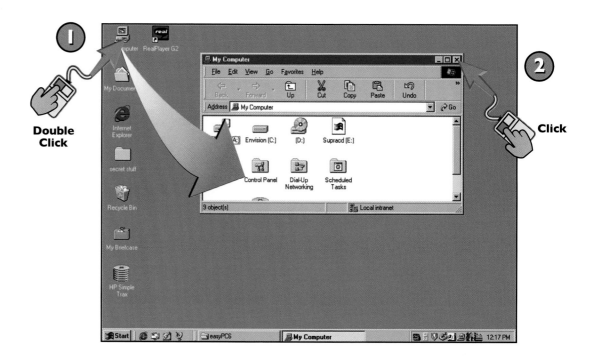

Double Click

Click

 Double-click the **My Computer** icon. A window opens.

 Click the **Close button** (marked with an **X**) on the end of the *title bar*. The window closes.

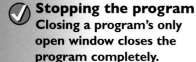 **Stopping the program**
Closing a program's only open window closes the program completely.

End Task

Task 10: Selecting a Window

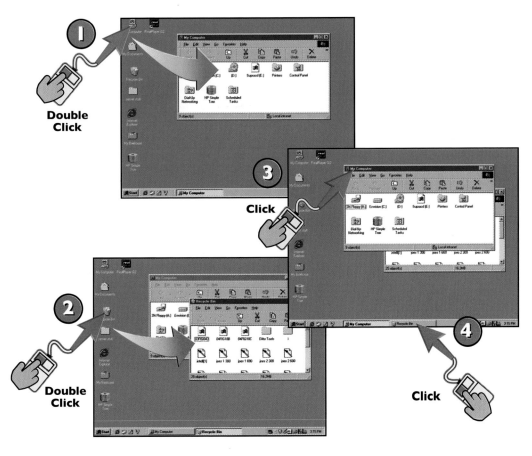

Double Click

Double Click

Click

Click

Selecting

One of Windows' best features is its capability to let you work on more than one program at a time. When you have more than one window open, however, you need to tell the computer with which window you want to work. When you *select* a window, Windows directs your commands to that program.

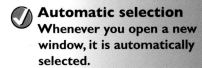

✓ **Automatic selection**
Whenever you open a new window, it is automatically selected.

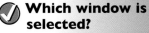

✓ **Which window is selected?**
The selected window's title bar is the brightest, and its taskbar button is depressed.

① Double-click the **My Computer** icon. A window opens.

② Double-click the **Recycle Bin** icon. A window opens.

③ Click the **title bar** of the My Computer window to select it.

④ Every open window has a button on the taskbar. Click one to select it.

End Task

Resizing

You can change the size of a window. You can make it larger so that you have more space to work in, or you can make it smaller, so that it's not covering up other things that you want to see on the screen. Most windows can be *resized* by using buttons in the title bar or by *dragging* the window's borders and corners.

Task 11: Resizing a Window

Click

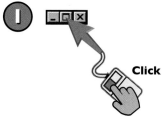

Click

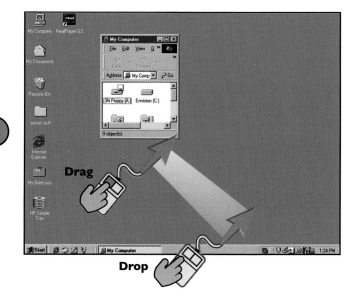

Drag

Drop

(✓) **Reduce or enlarge quickly**
Double-clicking the title bar can reduce a large window or enlarge a small one.

1 If the **Maximize button** is on the title bar, click it to expand the window to its largest size.

2 If the **Restore button** is on the title bar, click it to make the window smaller.

3 Point to a border or a corner of a window. If the pointer turns into a double-headed arrow, you can drag that border or corner into the window to make it smaller, or away to enlarge it.

End Task

Task 12: Moving a Window

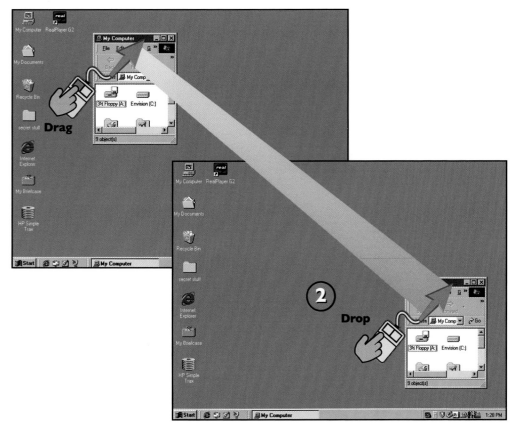

Drag

Drop

Moving a Window

You can move windows around the screen, which is useful if you're trying to arrange several windows so that you can see them all at once.

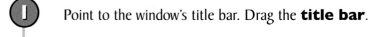

 Point to the window's title bar. Drag the **title bar**.

 When you release the mouse button, the window is in its new position.

✔ **What moves?**
Some Windows systems show the whole window while you drag it. With others, you drag a rectangular outline, and after you place the outline, the window moves into place.

PART 4

Minimizing a Window

If you're using several programs at the same time, your screen can become cluttered with Windows. You can hide some of those windows without closing the programs. To hide a window, you minimize it; every minimized window has a button on the taskbar.

✓ **Hide all the windows**
On some systems, you can click the **Show Desktop** button on the taskbar to minimize every window at once.

Task 13: Hiding a Window

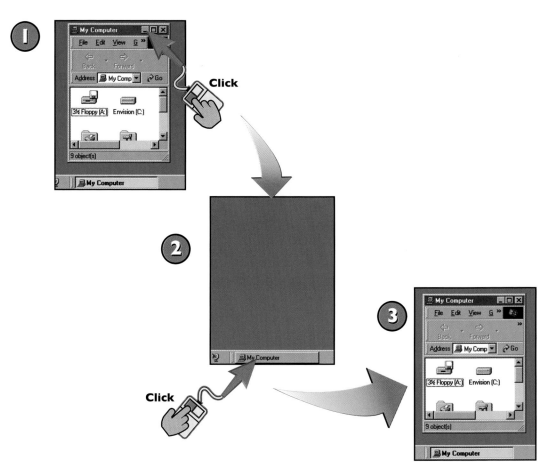

1 Click the *Minimize button* on the title bar.

2 The window disappears from the screen, but there's still a taskbar button for it. Click the taskbar button.

3 The window reappears.

Task 14: Understanding Scrollbars

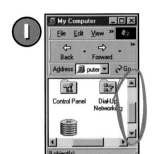

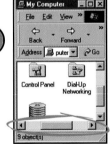

What Is a Scrollbar?

Sometimes, Windows has a larger image to show you than it can fit in the window. When that happens, you see just a part of what Windows wants to show you, plus *scrollbars*, which let you select the portion of the window you want to see.

The height of the scrollbar represents the height of the whole document.

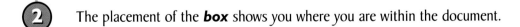
The placement of the *box* shows you where you are within the document.

The size of the box indicates what portion of the entire document you're seeing. The smaller the box, the less you're seeing.

Horizontal scrollbars appear when the document is wider than can be displayed.

 Want to try this?
To experiment with scrollbars, double-click the **My Computer** icon and shrink the window until the scrollbars appear.

Scrolling

When you scroll something, the image moves by smoothly. This is handy when you're searching for something within the document.

Task 15: Scrolling Through Your Document

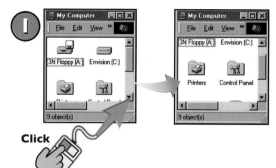

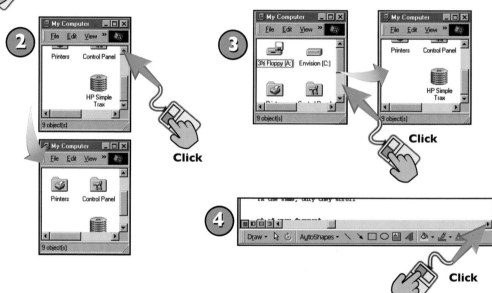

✓ **Continuous scrolling**
If you hold the mouse button down instead of just clicking, the scrolling continues until you release the button.

✓ **Scroll with your keyboard**
The Page Up key scrolls the document up. The Page Down key scrolls it down.

1. Click the **down** button to scroll to a lower part of the image.

2. Click the **up** button to scroll to a higher part of the image.

3. Click the scrollbar above the box to scroll up a whole window's worth, or below the box to scroll down a window's worth.

4. Horizontal scrollbars work the same, except they scroll left and right.

Task 16: Jumping to Another Part of Your Document

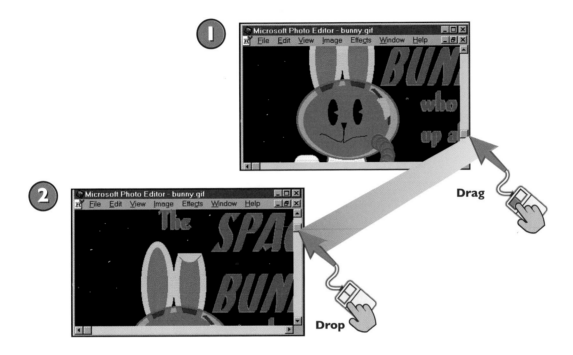

Drag

Drop

Scrolling Faster

You can use the scrollbar to quickly get to a specific place in the displayed item, without having to scroll through all the places in between.

1. Point to the box. Drag it up or down the scrollbar to the place that represents the area of the image that you want to see.

2. When you release the mouse button, the proper area of the image is displayed.

The Mouse Wheel

If your mouse has a wheel on the top of it, you can use this wheel to scroll up or down through the selected window without moving your pointer.

Task 17: Using the Mouse Wheel

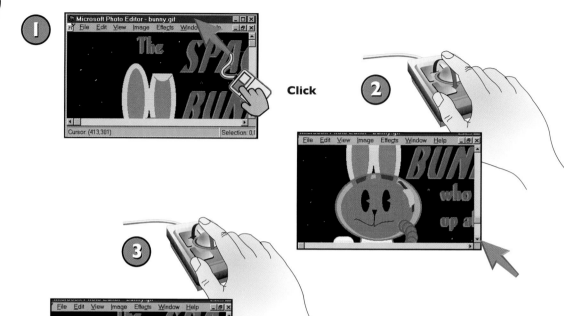

Click

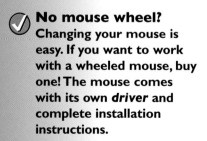

✓ **No mouse wheel?**
Changing your mouse is easy. If you want to work with a wheeled mouse, buy one! The mouse comes with its own *driver* and complete installation instructions.

 Make sure that the window you want to scroll is selected.

 Rolling the top of the wheel towards you scrolls down through the image.

 Rolling the top of the wheel away from you scrolls up through the image.

Task 18: Using a Menu

Start Here

Click

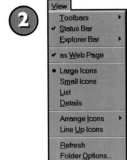

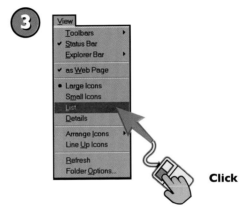

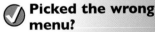

Click

Menus

Most program windows have a *menu bar*, a list of categories of commands, right under the title bar. You choose categories and commands by clicking them.

✓ **Picked the wrong menu?**
If you click the wrong command category, just point to the right one, and that menu opens.

✓ **Don't want a menu?**
If you didn't mean to open a menu, click the command category again to close it.

① On the *menu bar*, choose the category of the command that you want.

② The menu opens.

③ Choose the command you want.

End Task

Task 19: Using a Submenu

Submenus

Some of the items on menus aren't commands. Instead, they're a subcategory of commands. Selecting these brings up another menu, called the *submenu*.

Start Here

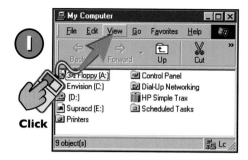

Click

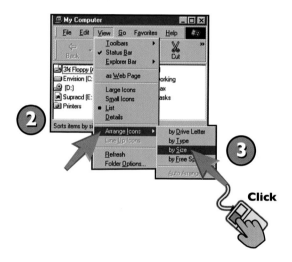

Click

✓ **Menu notation**
In this book, menu commands are listed by the menu category, the item from the menu, and the item from the submenu (if any). For example, choose **View, Arrange Icons, By Size**.

✓ **Grayed out**
If a menu command is in light type, you can't use it at this time.

1 Choose the category of the command that you want.

2 Point to a menu item with an arrow at the end, and a submenu appears.

3 Choose the command that you want.

End Task

Task 20: Using Shortcut Menus

Start Here

Right
Click

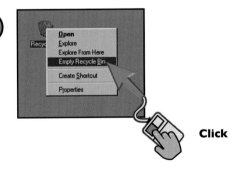

Click

Shortcut Menus

Many items on your screen have hidden menus that can be quickly opened at any time. These are called **_shortcut menus_**.

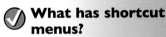 **What has shortcut menus?**
Every object on your Windows desktop has a shortcut menu, and many items in individual windows do, too.

✓ **Shortcut submenus**
Some shortcut menus have submenus.

✓ **Closing shortcut menus**
If you accidentally open a shortcut menu, just click anywhere else to close it.

1 Right-click the item for which you want a menu.

2 The shortcut menu appears.

3 Choose the command you want.

Typing

**Not everything can be done
with the mouse. The
keyboard is needed to type
in information. It works a
lot like a typewriter
keyboard, but it has some
additional functions.**

Task 21: Typing

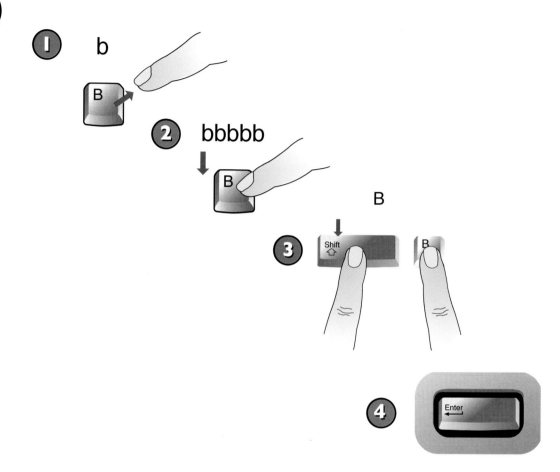

Start Here

① b

② bbbbb

③ Shift ⇧ / B

④ Enter

⚠ **WARNING**
**Avoid typing a lowercase L
instead of the number one,
or a capital 0 for zero. The
computer treats them very
differently.**

✓ **Double-character keys**
**Keys with two characters
on them give you the
lower character. To get the
upper character, press the
Shift key.**

① Press a key and release it quickly to get the letter or number pictured on the key.

② Holding down a key has the same effect as hitting it repeatedly.

③ Hold down the **Shift** key and tap a letter to get the capital letter.

④ When you've typed to the end of a line, the PC automatically detects it and starts a new line.
At the end of each paragraph, press **Enter** to insert a blank line and start a new paragraph.

End Task

Task 22: Using Combination Keys

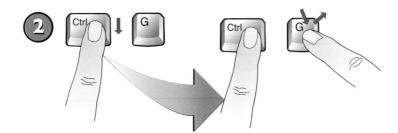

Combination Keys

Programs that use typed commands may have more commands than there are keys. To be able to handle additional commands, your keyboard uses *combination keys*—special keys that are designed to be used together with other keys to produce typed commands.

 A rare key
Not all keyboards have the Windows key. The key is marked with an image of the Windows logo, the Flying Window.

 The name of the keys
Ctrl is short for control. *Alt* is short for alternate.

 Shift, Alt, Ctrl, and Windows keys are found to either side of the Spacebar. They're used in combination with other keys.

 To do the key combination Ctrl+G (for example), hold down the **Ctrl** key and press and release the **G** key.

 Release the **Ctrl** key.

Task 23: Typing Menu Commands

Keyboard Control

You can issue commands from the menus by using the keyboard. This way, if you're typing something, you don't have to take your hand away from the keyboard to use the mouse.

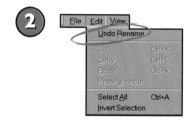

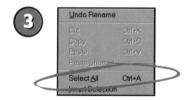

① Choose a menu by pressing **Alt+**the underlined letter in the command category name.

② Choose a command from the menu by typing the underlined letter in that command.

 Start menu shortcut
Press **Alt+Esc** to open the Start menu.

③ Some commands have shortcut keystrokes listed (such as Ctrl+A). Press this keystroke to use this command without going through menus.

Task 24: Using Caps Lock and Num Lock Keys

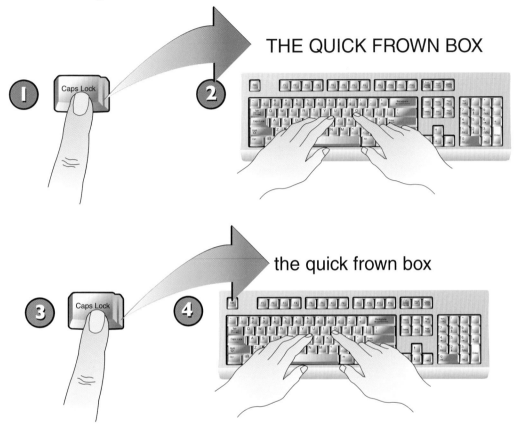

THE QUICK FROWN BOX

the quick frown box

Caps Lock and Num Lock

The Caps Lock and Num Lock keys change the function of other keys on your keyboard. The Caps Lock key switches you between typing in **ALL CAPITALS** and in lowercase. The Num Lock key switches the right-hand keypad between typing numbers and being used as cursor keys.

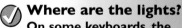

Where are the lights?
On some keyboards, the lights that indicate when the Caps Lock and Num Lock keys are pressed are on the keys themselves. On others, they are in a group of lights near an edge of the keyboard.

(1) Press **Caps Lock** to activate the Caps Lock mode.

(2) Now when you type, everything is in uppercase.

(3) Press **Caps Lock** again to turn the Caps Lock off.

(4) Typing has returned to normal.

Task 25: Using Cursor Keys

Cursor Keys

The cursor keys are used mainly when typing. You use them to move to a different point in what has been typed to make changes or corrections.

① The **cursor** is an onscreen bar that shows you where you're typing.

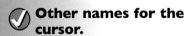

② When the Num Lock is off, some keys on the numeric keypad work as cursor keys. The arrow on the keys shows you the direction in which it moves the cursor.

③ Most keyboards have a separate set of cursor keys.

Next Step

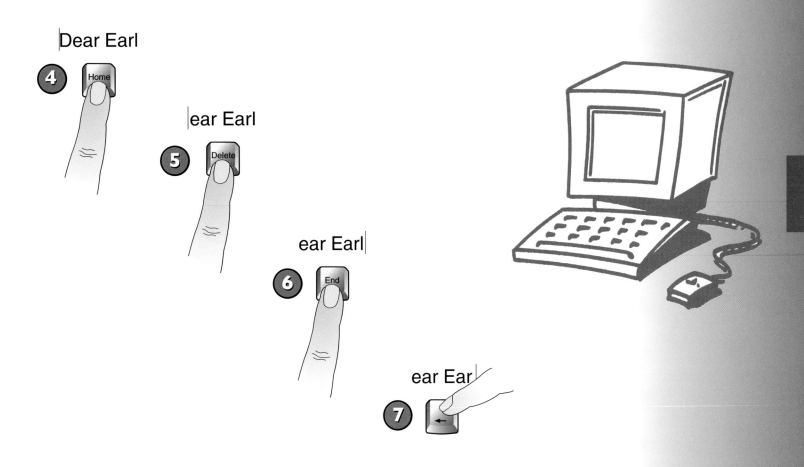

Dear Earl

4 Home

ear Earl

5 Delete

ear Earl

6 End

ear Ear

7

4 The Home key moves the cursor to the beginning of the line of text.

5 The Delete key removes the character after the cursor.

6 The End key moves the cursor to the end of the line of text.

7 The Backspace key (above the Enter key) removes the character before the cursor.

End
Task

Task 26: Finding Other Special Keys

Other Special Keys

The standard Windows keyboard has a number of other keys with their own special uses.

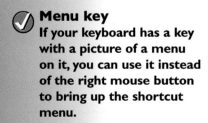

✓ **Menu key**
If your keyboard has a key with a picture of a menu on it, you can use it instead of the right mouse button to bring up the shortcut menu.

✓ **Other keys**
There are other keys with funky names or symbols that aren't described here. Different programs use these keys in various ways.

1 Press the **Esc** (escape) key to close and open menus, and to get yourself out of other situations that you didn't want to get into.

2 *Function keys* (sometimes called *F keys*) are used as command keys, with the command set by the program.

3 The slash key is used as the division sign, as in 6/2=3.

4 The star key is used as the multiplication sign, as in 3*2=6.

Task 27: Closing a Windows Program

Start Here

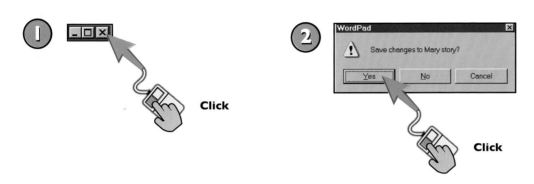

Click

Click

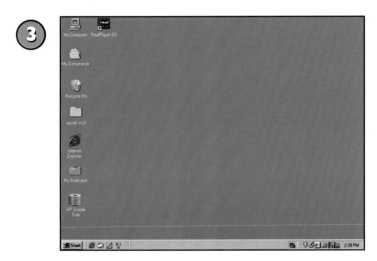

After You've Finished

When you're finished using a program, you shouldn't leave it open. It may be taking up memory that another program needs. When you *close* a program, you're telling the computer that you're finished with it.

① Click the Close button (**X**) in the title bar of the program's window.

② If you have not saved the work you've done, the program asks you whether you want to. Click **Yes** to save it, or **No** to lose everything you've done.

③ The program window disappears. The program is now closed.

✓ **Exiting via menu**
If the close button is grayed out, try choosing the menu command **File, Exit**.

✓ **Exiting via keyboard**
The keyboard shortcut for closing a program is **Alt+F4**.

End Task

PART 5

Interacting with Windows

In this section, you learn how to use and communicate information to the Windows operating system. In Windows, you use dialog boxes to communicate commands, option choices, and other information to programs and Windows. You use My Computer to find files, copy them, rename them, and get rid of them when you don't need them any more. This part also covers things that make working with Windows more comfortable—things like setting up the mouse to work well with your hand, setting up a screen saver to add some decoration to your computer, and even using your PC to play CDs so that you can listen to music while you work!

Tasks

Task 1: Understanding Dialog Boxes

What Is a Dialog Box?

A *dialog box* is a window that enables you to choose options and send other information to a program. The content of dialog boxes varies, depending on the type of information that the dialog box is requesting.

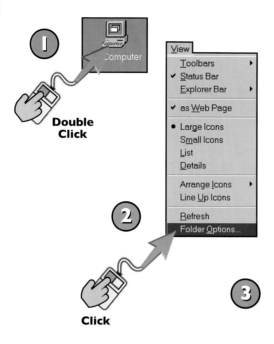

Double
Click

Click

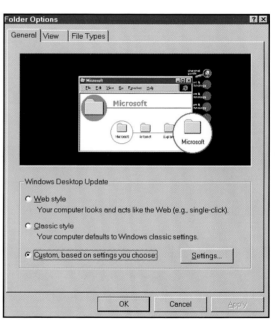

1 To see an example of a dialog box, double-click **My Computer**.

2 Choose **View**, **Folder Options**.

3 The Folder Options dialog box opens. It has examples of some (but not all) dialog box features.

Task 2: Selecting Options in a Dialog Box

Start Here

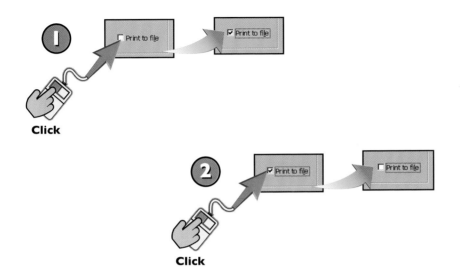

Click

Click

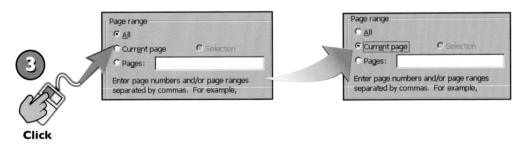

Click

Option Buttons and Checkboxes

Many dialog boxes present a list of simple choices; they ask you to choose Yes or No or to select from a small list of options. You can use *option buttons* or *checkboxes* to make such simple selections with a single click.

 You can't choose these
If the checkbox or option button is the same color as the background of the dialog box (*grayed out*), that means the option is not currently available.

 Using default settings
All dialog box options are automatically set to some default value, and often the default setting is the best. If you want that default value, just leave it there!

① A **checkbox** is used to activate or deactivate an option—like a yes-or-no choice. Click an empty checkbox to put a check in it and to activate the option.

② Clicking a selected checkbox removes the check and deactivates the option.

③ To choose from a set of several options, click the **option button** for the option you want. The dot marks the selected option.

End Task

Task 3: Using Dialog Box Lists

Start
Here

Lists

When you have several options to choose from, the dialog box displays one of two sorts of lists: a *scrollable list* or a *drop-down list.*

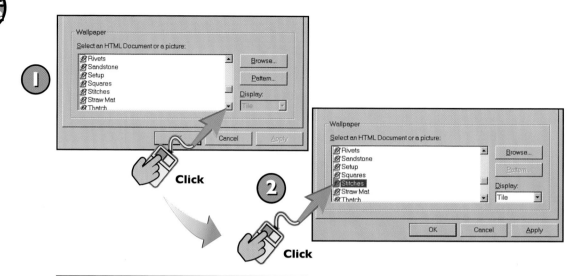

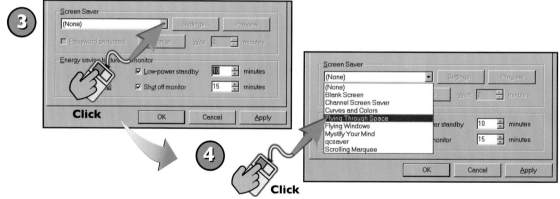

(1) To select an item from a *scrollable list*, use the scrollbar to find the choice you want.

(2) Click your choice.

(3) To see the choices on a *drop-down list*, click the drop-down arrow.

(4) Click your choice.

End
Task

Task 4: Entering Words and Numbers in a Dialog Box

Start Here

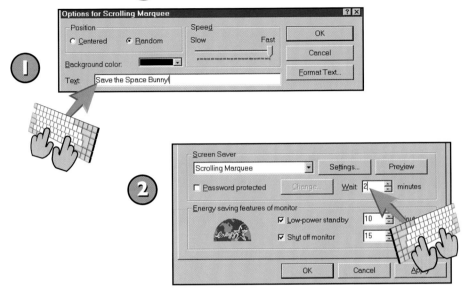

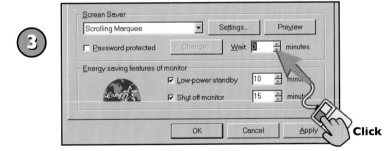
Click

① To enter text, click the text box. Type your text.

② You can use a numeric field the same way you use a text box.

③ You can also use the arrow buttons to increase or decrease the value.

Text and Numbers

Dialog boxes often have a space to type in text (called a *text box* or text field) or a number (a numeric box or numeric field). When you're working in one of these boxes, you can use the cursor keys to edit the information that you've typed.

✓ **Drop-down lists**
Some text boxes include a drop-down list from which you can select typed text. Click the drop-down arrow to review the list, and click an item in the list to select it.

✓ **The pointer changes**
When you point to a text or number field, your pointer changes from an arrow to an I shape.

End Task

Task 5: Using a Slider

Sliders

A *slider* lets you select one of a range of values. For example, a computer chess program may have a slider that lets you choose a level of playing expertise, with one end of the slider marked "very easy" and the other marked "very difficult." You could drag the slider to any point between those extremes, to set the playing level of your choice.

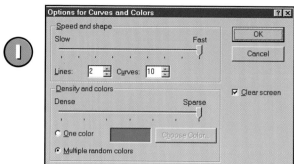

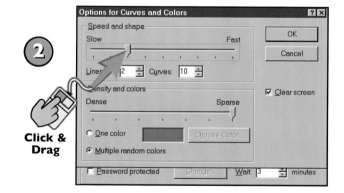

Click & Drag

(1) The range is marked on the ends of the slider.

(2) Drag the slider to the point representing the value you want.

Task 6: Using Dialog Box Tabs

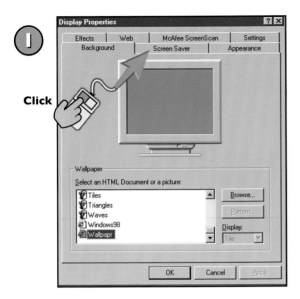

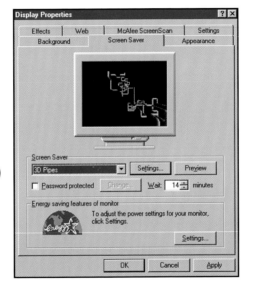

Tabs

Some dialog boxes have options for more than one category of information. Rather than displaying all the options at once, each category is put on a _tab_ that you can select to view and choose those options.

 The categories are described on tabs near the top of the dialog box. Click the category that you want.

 The setting fields for that category appear. You can set the options on this tab and then click on another tab to set options there.

 Tab examples
To see the dialog box used in this example, right-click a blank part of the desktop and choose Properties from the shortcut menu.

Task 7: Closing a Dialog Box

Start Here

Done with the Box?

When you're finished using the dialog box, just click a button to let the program know you're done.

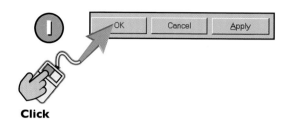

Click

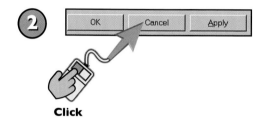

Click

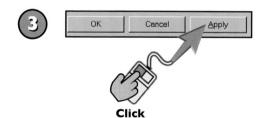

Click

✓ **Closing from the keyboard**
Pressing **Enter** has the same effect as clicking OK.

✓ **Working with multiple tabs**
OK and Apply set all the settings in a dialog box, not just the ones on the current tab.

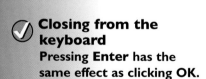

1. Choosing **OK** closes the dialog box. The computer then acts on the options you set.

2. Choosing **Cancel** closes the dialog box and tells the computer not to act on the options you set.

3. Choosing **Apply** tells the computer to act on the options that you set without closing the dialog box.

End Task

Task 8: Using a File Dialog Box

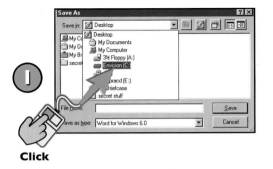

Click

Double Click

Double Click

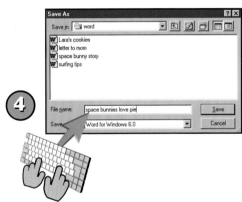

Storing and Retrieving a File

When you save a file for the first time, you have to indicate to the program where to store the saved file. When you want to open a saved file, you have to indicate where the file is stored for the program to find and open it. When you give a program a command to open or save a document, the program displays a *file dialog box* designed for this purpose.

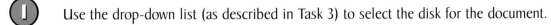

✅ **Already in the folder?**
If the file dialog box displays the right folder to begin with, skip steps 1 and 2.

✅ **File of a certain type?**
Some programs can load or save several different types of files. Use the bottom drop-down list to select the type you want.

① Use the drop-down list (as described in Task 3) to select the disk for the document.

② Double-click the folder in which the document is saved, or the folder in which you want to save the document (repeat this step to reach a subfolder).

③ To open an existing document, double-click the document's icon.

④ To save a new document, type a name for the document and then press **Enter**.

Task 9: Getting Help with a Dialog Box

Using the What's This? Tool

Sometimes, you may need more information about the options presented to you in a dialog box. If the dialog box offers the What's This? question mark on its title bar, you can use it to get help information specific to the fields in that dialog box.

Click

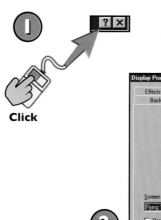

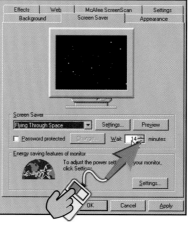

Click

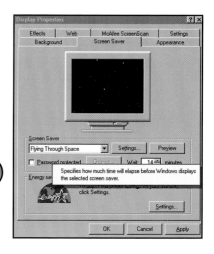

 No help?
Not all dialog boxes have this feature.

 Help from the keyboard
You can get the help information on the currently highlighted field by pressing the **F1** key.

Clicking the **What's This?** button changes the pointer to an arrow with a question mark next to it.

Use this pointer to click the field on which you want information.

When the information appears, the standard pointer is restored. Click anywhere to get rid of the information.

Task 10: Opening Windows Help

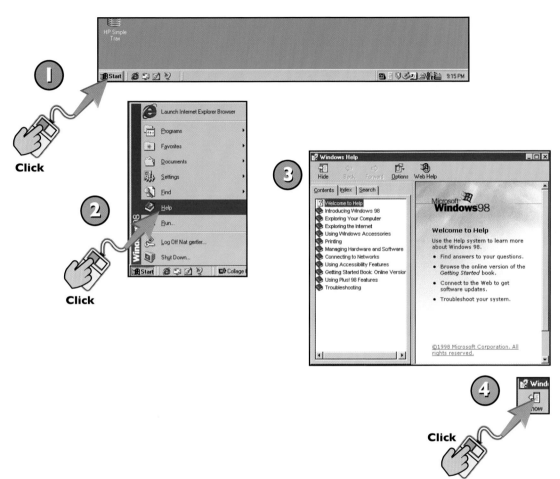

Click

Click

Click

Start Here

The Windows Help System

Windows keeps a manual of helpful information about the operating system on your hard disk. Although it's not a complete reference work, it can answer a lot of simple questions.

① Click **Start**.

② Click **Help**.

③ The Help system opens. The tabs on the dialog box offer three methods of looking through the Help information: a table of contents, an index, and a word-search tool.

④ If you don't see the tabs for these items, click the **Show** button.

✓ Help from the keyboard
If you don't have any windows selected, you can press **F1** to open the Help system.

Finding Help by Category

The Help information in the Contents tab of the Windows Help feature is organized into books and categories. A book is a collection of categories and often has other books within it. A category is the actual document that contains the Help information.

Task 11: Browsing the Contents of Windows Help

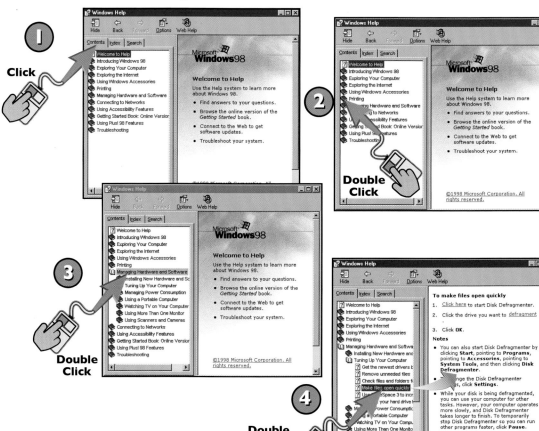

Click

Double Click

Double Click

Double Click

① Click **Contents**.

② If you want to see the contents of a book, double-click it.

③ Repeat step 2 for books-within-books until you see a category you want.

④ Double-click the category on which you want information, and the information appears.

Task 12: Searching the Help Index

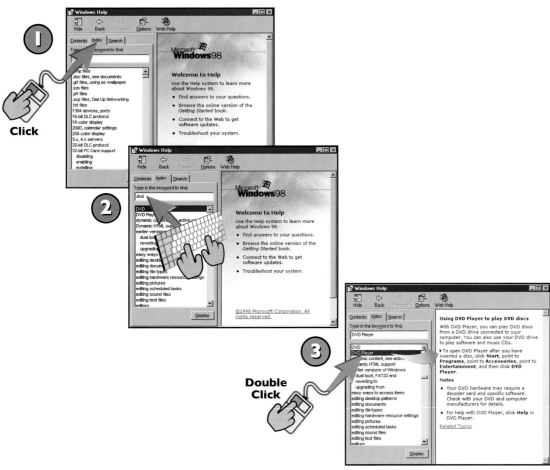

Click

Double Click

Help Index

The Help Index is like the index in this book, enabling you to quickly find information about a specific topic.

 No help?
If the index doesn't find anything for the topic you entered, try another word that means the same thing.

 Subtopics
Selecting certain topics brings up a list of subtopics. Double-click a subtopic to open the Help information.

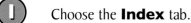

1 Choose the **Index** tab.

2 Type the first few letters of the topic for which you're looking, and the index scrolls to that point in the alphabetic list.

3 Double-click the topic you want, and the Help information appears.

Task 13: Using the Help Information

The Help Display

The Help information is usually step-by-step instructions indicating how to do what you want. It often has things you can click to get more information or to get the computer to take some of the steps for you.

 Start Here

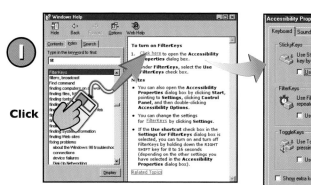

Click

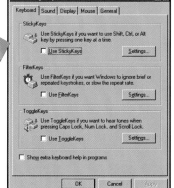

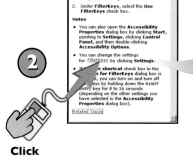

Click

 Click

 Click

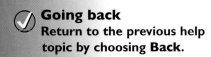 **Going back**
Return to the previous help topic by choosing **Back.**

1. Click an arrow button or a Click Here link, and the program mentioned in the information will start.

2. Click an underlined word, and a definition of that word pops up.

3. Many Help topics have buttons that link to other Help files or topic menus.

 End Task

Task 14: Getting Help with a Program

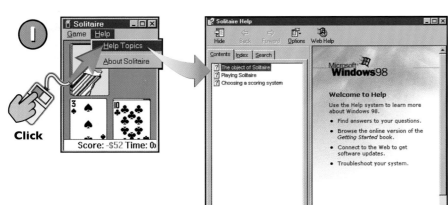

Click

Program Help

Most programs have some sort of Help information built in. Many of them use the same system that the main Windows Help uses.

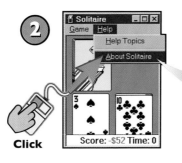

Click

① Choose the **Help** menu. The first command on the Help menu usually brings up the program's main Help system.

② The last command on the Help menu usually brings up revision, copyright, and more about the making of the program.

 Help from the keyboard
Pressing **F1** opens Help information in most programs.

Task 15: Browsing Through Your Files

Opening a File Browser

The **My Computer** desktop icon is your gateway to finding all the files stored on your computer. Opening My Computer starts a *file browser*, a program that enables you to view a list of files and folders on your disks.

✓ **Looks different?**
Your My Computer window may look quite different from these pictures, depending on your version of Windows and what you have selected on the View menu.

✓ **No toolbar?**
Choose **View, Toolbars, Standard Buttons** or just **View, Toolbar** (depending on your Windows setup).

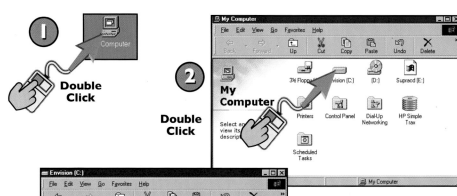

Double Click

Double Click

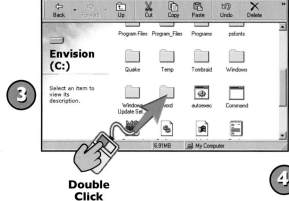

Double Click

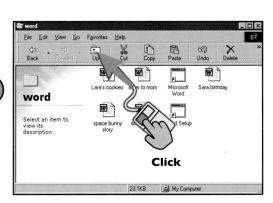

Click

Start Here

1. Double-click **My Computer**.

2. Double-click the icon for your hard disk to see a list of files and folders in the root folder.

3. Double-click a folder icon to see a list of files and folders in that folder.

4. Click the **Up** button to get back to the folder containing this folder.

End Task

Task 16: Opening a Document File

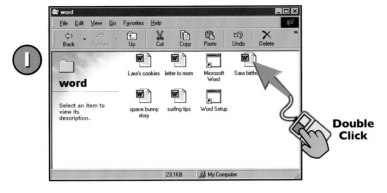

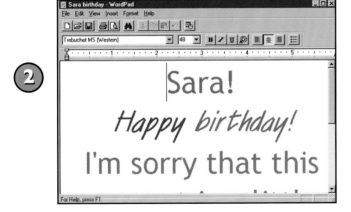

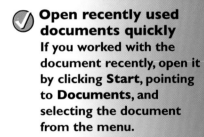

Every File Is Associated with a Program

Windows keeps track of what kind of document—word processing, spreadsheet, database, and so on—each file holds. When you open a file, Windows automatically loads and launches the program in which the file was created or another program that can read and display that document.

✓ **Open recently used documents quickly**
If you worked with the document recently, open it by clicking **Start**, pointing to **Documents**, and selecting the document from the menu.

✓ **Wrong program?**
To open a document from within a program, start the program you want and use the **File, Open** command to open the document.

① Use My Computer to locate the file you want to open and then double-click the file.

② The program opens, displaying the document.

③ If the icon looks like this, Windows doesn't know which program goes with this document. Start the program, and use the **File, Open** command to open this document.

Task 17: Opening a Program

Opening

Opening a program means that the program starts running and opens a blank window. Usually, you open a program using the Start menu (shown in Part 4, Task 6). Occasionally, however, you have to start a program that hasn't been installed on your PC already (for example, starting the program that installs a program), and that's when you'd use this method.

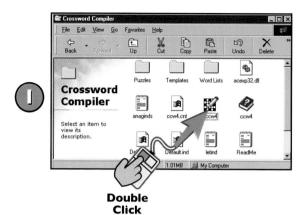

Double Click

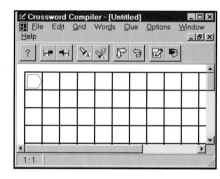

 Find the program in the file browser (as shown in Task 15) and double-click it.

Ⓑ The program opens.

End Task

Task 18: Creating a New Folder

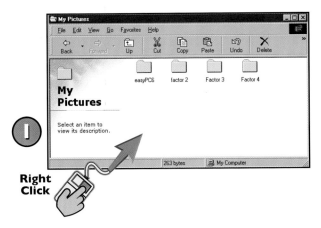

Right Click

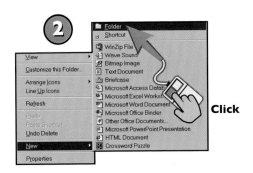

Click

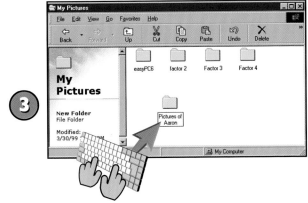

New Folders

You use folders to organize files so that you can quickly find them. Folders can contain both files and other folders (subfolders). For example, you may have a folder that contains all your Word documents. Within that folder, you may have a subfolder just for letters, and the Letters subfolder may contain yet another subfolder just for letters to Mom.

1. In My Computer, open the folder within which you want to create a new subfolder. Right-click a blank area in the window.

2. Choose **New**, **Folder**, and a new folder appears.

3. Type a name for the folder.

End Task

Task 19: Moving a Document

Moving Documents

The main reason to move documents from one folder to another is to reorganize your documents, making it easier to find the one you want.

Right Click

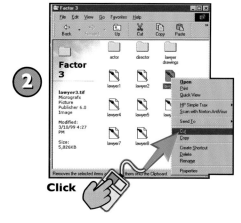

Click

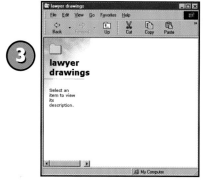

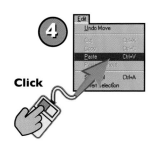

Click

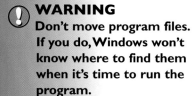

⚠ WARNING
Don't move program files. If you do, Windows won't know where to find them when it's time to run the program.

✔ Short moves
To move a document from its folder to a subfolder in that folder, drag the document's icon and drop it on the subfolder's icon.

① Right-click the icon for the document you want to move.

② Select **Cut** from the shortcut menu. The file icon appears to be faded.

③ Browse to the folder you want to move the document into, as shown in Task 15.

④ Open the **Edit** menu and choose **Paste**.

End Task

Task 20: Copying Files

Start Here

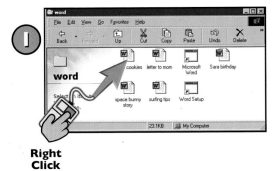

Right Click

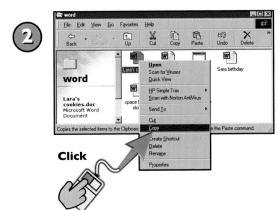

Click

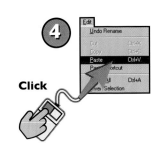

Click

Making Copies

There are many times when copying files is handy. For example, you might want to copy a file from your hard disk onto a floppy so you can give it to someone else. Or you might make a copy of a letter you wrote to Mom so you can make a few changes to it and send the same letter to Grampa.

(1) Right-click the icon for the document you want to copy.

(2) Select **Copy** from the shortcut menu.

(3) Browse to the folder you want to copy the document to, as shown in Task 15.

(4) Open the **Edit** menu and choose **Paste**.

✅ **Copy everything in the folder**
Press **Ctrl+A** to highlight all the contents in the current folder, then go on to step 1.

End Task

Page
113

Task 21: Printing Documents

Using the Printer

Having a document on the computer can be very handy. You can read it all you want on the computer screen, make changes to it, even email it to someone. If you want a copy to stick in your back pocket or to mail off to Aunt Lorna, you have to print the document onto paper.

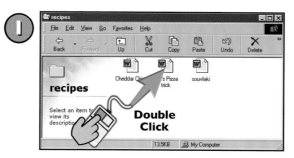

Double Click

Click

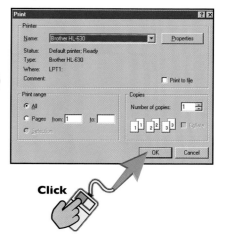

Click

✓ **Click the Print button**
Most programs have a Print button with a picture of a printer; click it to print a copy of the current document.

✓ **Other print options**
Every program's Print dialog box has different options that you can select. Most let you print multiple copies or print one part of a large document.

1. Double-click the document icon to open the document.

2. Choose **File**, **Print**.

3. Click **OK** in the Print dialog box, and the file prints.

Task 22: Deleting Documents

Start Here

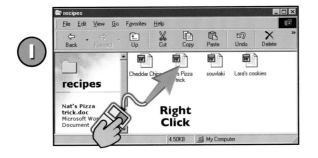

Right Click

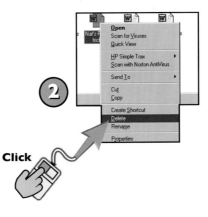

Click

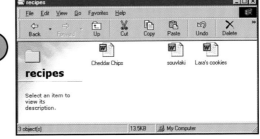

Click

Getting Rid of Old Documents

It's a good idea to delete files when you're sure that you aren't going to need them anymore. Deleting them makes room on your disk for more files.

① Right-click the icon for the document that you want to delete.

② Choose **Delete**.

③ On the dialog box that appears, choose **Yes**.

④ The document is now deleted.

✔ **Delete a whole folder**
You can delete entire folders using the same technique shown for a document. When you delete a folder, it and all its contents are sent to the Recycle Bin.

⚠ **WARNING**
Don't delete program files. If you want to get rid of a program, uninstall it (see Part 6, Task 10).

End Task

Page
115

Task 23: Undeleting Documents

Recovering Deleted Files

Because people sometimes accidentally delete the wrong file, Windows temporarily stores all the deleted files in an area called the *Recycle Bin* so that you can retrieve them.

Start Here

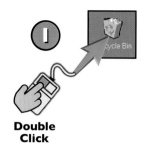
Double Click

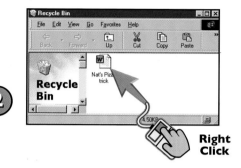
Right Click

Click

✓ Undelete several at once

In step 2, while holding down **Ctrl**, click each of the files that you want to undelete.

⚠ WARNING

Be careful when using someone else's PC! Some people set up their PC so that deleted files are removed immediately, and cannot be undeleted.

1. Double-click the **Recycle Bin** icon on the desktop.

2. Right-click the icon for the file that you want to undelete.

3. Choose **Restore**.

4. The file is moved from the Recycle Bin back to where it was when you deleted it.

End Task

Task 24: Emptying the Recycle Bin

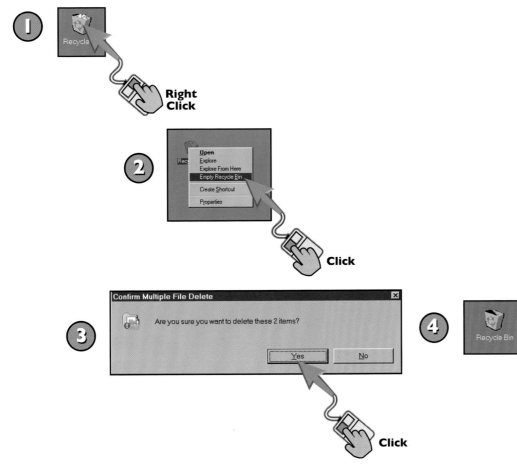

Right Click

Open
Explore
Explore From Here
Empty Recycle Bin
Create Shortcut
Properties

Click

Confirm Multiple File Delete

Are you sure you want to delete these 2 items?

Yes   No

Click

Recycle Bin

Getting More Disk Space

The deleted files are still taking up space on your disk until you empty the Recycle Bin. When you empty the Recycle Bin, the space is freed up—but all the files that were in the Recycle Bin are gone for good.

✓ Anything to empty?
When files are in the Recycle Bin, the icon looks like a full wastebasket. When the Recycle Bin has no files, it looks empty.

⊘ WARNING
After you empty the Recycle Bin, all those deleted files are gone. They cannot be undeleted.

1 Right-click the **Recycle Bin** icon.

2 Choose **Empty Recycle Bin**.

3 Click **Yes**.

4 The files are erased from the disk, and the icon changes to look like an empty wastebasket.

Task 25: Creating a Shortcut

Shortcuts

A shortcut is an icon that you create on your desktop and use to open a folder, document, or program directly from the desktop (without having to go through My Computer). An icon for the document is still in My Computer; the new icon is a shortcut.

Start Here

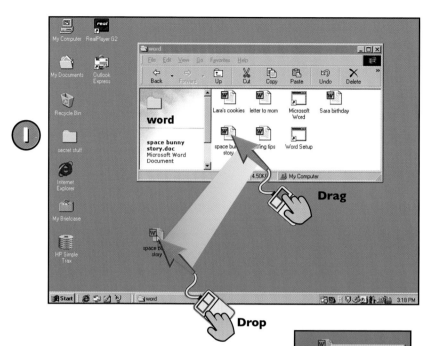

Drag

Drop

Move Here
Copy Here
Create Shortcut(s) Here
Cancel

Click

Double Click

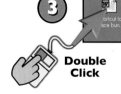

✓ Shortcut on the Start menu
To place a shortcut on the Start menu, hold down **Shift+Ctrl** and drag the file's icon onto the Start button.

✓ Recognizing shortcuts
You can distinguish a shortcut icon by the arrow in its lower-left corner.

1. In My Computer, find the document's icon and, while holding down the *right* mouse button (instead of the usual left), drag the file's icon to the desktop.

2. Release the icon, and a menu appears. Choose **Create Shortcut(s) Here**.

3. To use the shortcut, double-click it.

End Task

Task 26: Playing Music CDs

Start Here

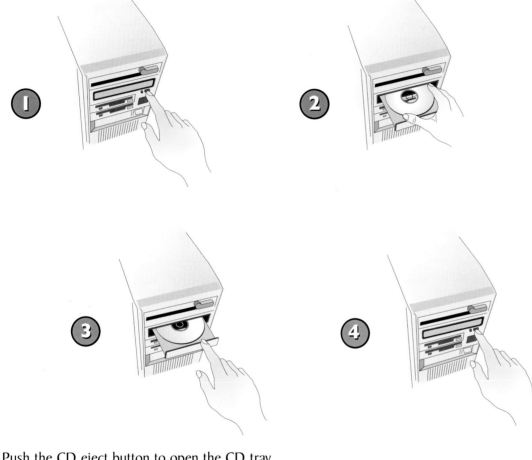

Music Discs

If you have a **CD-ROM** drive, it can play audio CDs through the speakers, so you can listen to music while you work.

✅ **If this doesn't work**
Check to be sure that your speakers are on. Next, from the **Start** menu, choose **Programs**, **Accessories**. In either the **Entertainment** or **Multimedia** submenu, choose **CD Player**. When the **CD Player** program opens, click the Play button to hear your music.

✅ **Use headphones**
Plug headphones into the jack in the front of your **CD-ROM** drive to keep your music to yourself.

① Push the CD eject button to open the CD tray.

② Put the CD into the empty tray.

③ Push the front of the tray slightly to close it. In a few seconds, the music starts playing.

④ When the CD has stopped playing, push the CD eject button to eject the tray and remove the CD.

End Task

Page
119

Task 27: Copying a Floppy Disk

Disk Duplication

By copying the contents of one floppy disk onto another disk, you can have a spare copy to give to someone. You can also use this as an emergency backup copy in case something goes wrong with your original floppy disk.

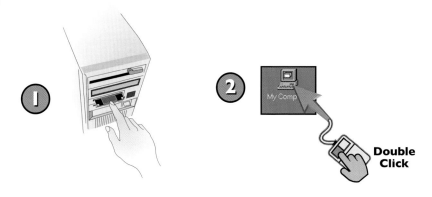

Double Click

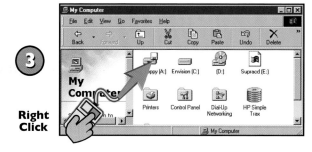

Right Click

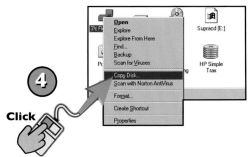

Click

(1) Insert into the floppy drive the disk that you want to copy.

(2) Double-click **My Computer**.

(3) Right-click the icon for your floppy drive.

(4) Choose **Copy Disk** from the shortcut menu.

Next Step

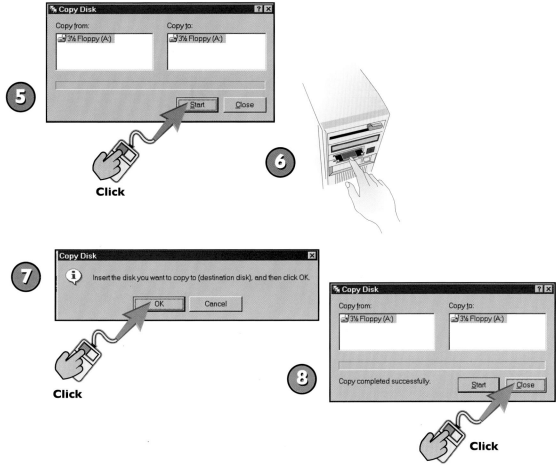

Click

Click

Click

(5) A Copy Disk dialog box appears. Click **Start** and wait while the PC reads all the information on your floppy.

(6) When a dialog box appears prompting you to insert the destination disk, replace the disk that's in the drive with a new disk.

(7) Click **OK**. The PC spends some time writing the data to the disk.

(8) When the copying is complete, click **Close**.

Task 28: Changing Your Mouse Speed

Adjusting the Mouse

Everyone's hands are different. Some people take more time to double-click than the system usually allows. Other people might want to make their mouse more sensitive, so the pointer zooms across the screen easily. You can use this task to adjust these mouse speeds so that the mouse is more comfortable to use.

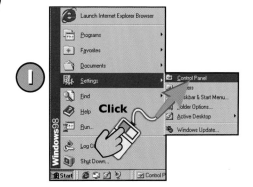

Double Click

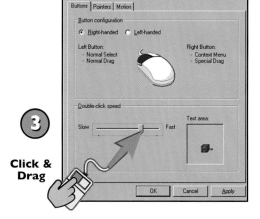

Click & Drag

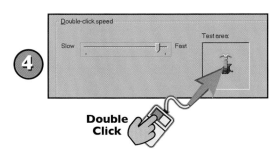

Double Click

✓ **Control Panel**
The other icons in the Control Panel can be used to customize Windows in many ways.

✓ **The right pointer speed**
If you set the pointer speed to move too fast, it is hard to put the pointer right where you want it. If you set it to move too slowly, it takes too much work to move the pointer across the screen.

① From the **Start** menu, choose **Settings**, **Control Panel**.

② Double-click the **Mouse** icon in the Control Panel. (You may need to scroll down to find it.)

③ Drag the **Double-click speed** slider to the point that represents how fast you double-click.

④ Double-click the **jack-in-the-box**. If he doesn't pop out, you've set your speed too fast. Repeat step 3.

Next Step

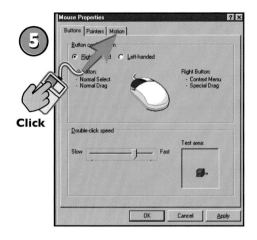

Click

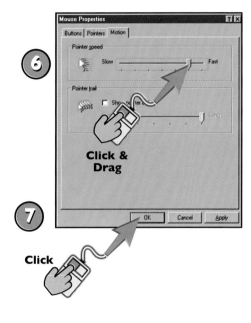

**Click &
Drag**

Click

5 Click the **Motion** tab.

6 Drag the **Pointer speed** slider to the point that represents how fast you want the pointer to move.

7 Click **OK**.

End
Task

Task 29: Setting Up for a Left-Handed User

The Left-Handed Mouse

Using a mouse with your left hand can be cumbersome, because your most agile finger isn't on the most-used button. With these steps, you switch the function of the buttons, so that the right button is used for clicking and double-clicking. The left button is used for right-clicking.

Start Here

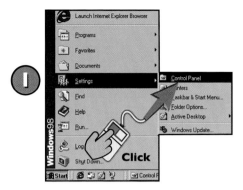

① Click

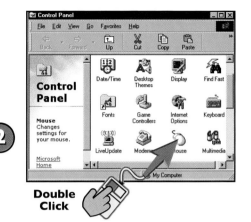

② Double Click

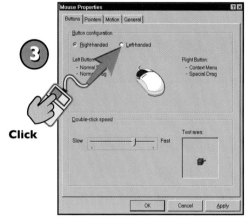

③ Click

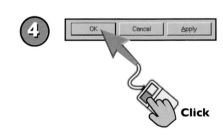

④ Click

✓ **Where does the mouse go?**
Remember to move the mouse to the left side of the keyboard, where it's easy to reach with the left hand.

① From the **Start** menu, choose **Settings**, **Control Panel**.

② Double-click the **Mouse** icon in the Control Panel. (You may need to scroll down to find it.)

③ Click **Left-handed**.

④ Click **OK**.

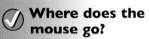

End Task

Task 30: Choosing Your Screen Saver

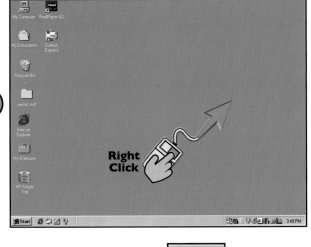

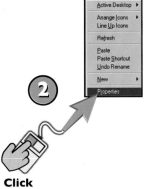

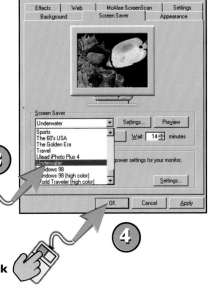

What's a Screen Saver?

A *screen saver* is a special program that starts up if you have not used your PC for several minutes. It displays a nifty, moving scene that fills your screen. The moment that you move your mouse or press a key, the screen saver disappears.

✓ **Screen saver options**
Each screen saver has its own options that change its appearance. Click the **Options** button on the **Screen Saver** tab to get a dialog box of options for the currently selected screen saver. Use the Preview in this dialog box to check out your choices.

✓ **Other screen savers**
You can buy interesting screen savers to add to your system, featuring popular licensed characters.

1. Right-click on a blank area of the desktop.

2. Click **Properties** to open the Display Properties dialog box.

3. On the **Screen Saver** tab, select a screen saver from the drop-down list. It is then displayed in the demo area.

4. Click **OK** to make this your screen saver.

Making Your PC Useful

You've seen how to set up your computer and work with it. Now it's time to get the computer to work for you. You do that by using programs. Many different types of programs are available. **Utilities**, for example, are programs designed to make your computer more efficient and easier to use by doing such things as speeding up your hard disk or preventing computer viruses. In this part of the book, we talk about **applications**—programs designed to help you do the work (and play!) you bought your PC to do.

In this part, you see what the most popular types of applications can do. So many varieties of each type of application can be found that this book cannot give you instructions for all of them, but you do see a sampling of application types and how they work.

Tasks

Task 1: Using a Word Processor

Creating Letters, Reports, and Other Documents

A *word processor* is a program that enables you to create letters, reports, stories, and any other kind of document you might have once created on a typewriter. Word processing programs are a lot more flexible than a typewriter because you can fix and change the text in your document before you print it.

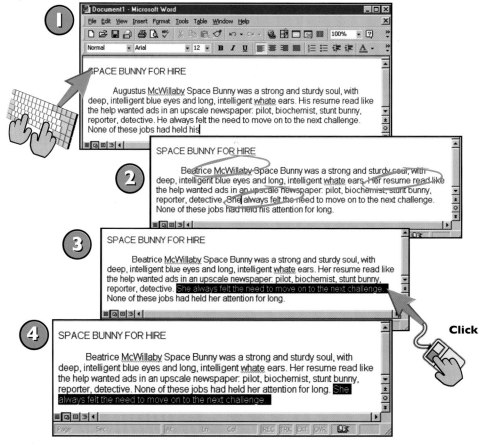

Start Here

Click

Popular word processors
The most popular word processors include **WordPerfect and Microsoft Word.**

1. Type the document.

2. Edit the document by moving the cursor through it, deleting words that you don't want and adding new ones that you do.

3. Select text to cut from one place.

4. Paste it in another.

Next Step

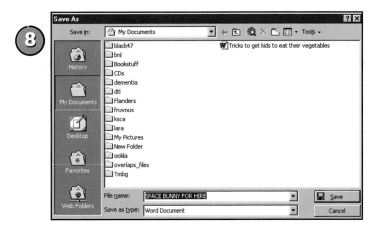

5 Use the word processor's **spell check** function to find words that may be misspelled. The program suggests words that you possibly meant to type.

6 Format your document, setting colors, font, and size for the text, as well as page **margins** (the distance from the edge of the paper to the point the text starts and ends).

7 Print your document by using your printer.

8 Save the document on your disk so that you can load it later to work on it.

End Task

Task 2: Using a Spreadsheet

Working with Numbers

A *spreadsheet* program can perform many mathematical calculations quickly, letting you work with large groups of numbers. It keeps track of all the numbers on a large grid, called a *spreadsheet* or a *worksheet*.

Spreadsheet programs can translate your data into charts and graphs and display them right in your worksheet or print them for reports.

✓ **Popular spreadsheets**
Lotus 1-2-3 and Microsoft Excel are the best-selling spreadsheet programs.

✓ **Use it as a database**
Most modern spreadsheets can also be used as simple database programs, with each column standing for a *field* and each row holding one *record*.

1 The spreadsheet is made up of numbered rows and lettered columns.

2 The rows and columns make up a grid of *cells*. Each cell is named for the column and row it is in, such as A3 or C17.

3 You can type numbers into the cells.

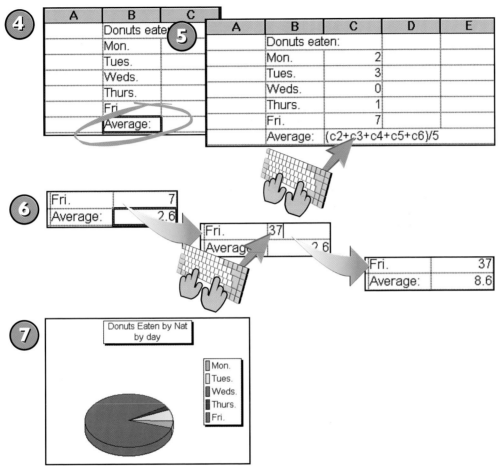

4️⃣ You can also type text (called **labels**) into the cells.

5️⃣ You can put in calculations based on the values in other cells. The program displays the result of the calculation.

6️⃣ Change one value, and the program automatically recalculates all the calculations around the new value.

7️⃣ The program can create graphs and charts based on the numbers.

Task 3: Using a Database

Managing Groups of Information

A *database program* is a program designed to keep track of lists of information (called *databases*). If you want to create an address book, a customer list, a catalog of your comic book collection, or a product inventory tracking form, a database is the program you want.

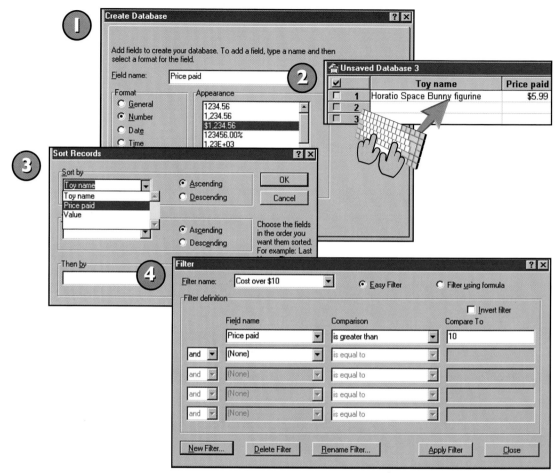

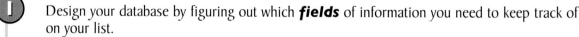

✓ **Popular database programs**
The most popular database programs these days are Access and FoxPro.

✓ **Specialty database programs**
Database programs are available for specific uses, such as tracking customer contacts or collecting baseball cards. The fields are all set up, making them easier to use.

(1) Design your database by figuring out which *fields* of information you need to keep track of on your list.

(2) Enter the *records*, the information in the fields for each item on your list.

(3) Manage your information by adding records, deleting recordings, and sorting them.

(4) Print a report listing all the records that meet criteria that you select, sorted in an order that you choose.

Task 4: Using Program Suites

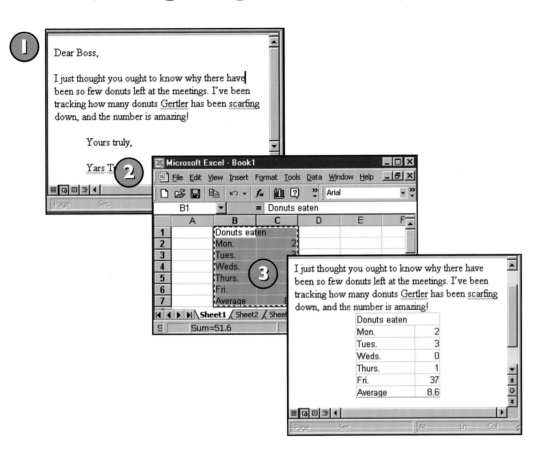

Working with a Family of Programs

A *program suite* is a group of programs designed to work together. They always include a word processor and a spreadsheet, and often include a database, a communications program, a schedule manager, or other programs. When you work with a program suite, you can create a single document that contains information created in each of the different programs.

① Popular suites
Microsoft Office, Lotus SmartSuite, and Corel WordPerfect Office are popular program suites. Microsoft Works, which is well designed for beginners, is available as part of Microsoft's Home Essentials pack.

① With a suite, you can create a word processor document…

② …and create a spreadsheet…

③ …and then combine them into a single document.

Creating Art on the PC

Computer technology has made completely new categories of art tools available and easy to use. *Paint* and *draw programs* enable you to create your images from scratch. *Photo enhancement programs* enable you to add visual effects to photographs, and *modeling programs* enable you to create three-dimensional images and effects. These and other computer art programs enable you to exercise your creativity and have fun!

✓ **Some popular computer art programs**
Paint is a simple paint program that comes as part of Windows. Adobe Illustrator, Kai's Power Goo, and TrueSpace are other computer art programs available today.

Task 5: Using Paint, Draw, and Other Computer Art Programs

Start Here

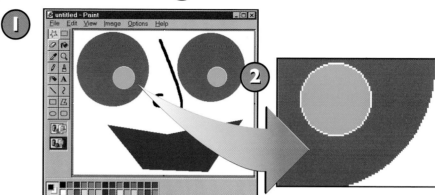

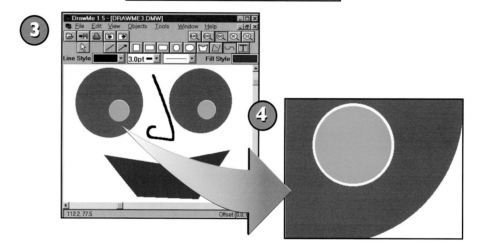

① A **paint program** lets you use your pointer like a pen or a brush to create images by applying colors to each pixel on the screen.

② If you enlarge a paint picture, you just get bigger dots.

③ A **draw program** enables you to build a picture as a series of lines, curves, and shapes.

④ Enlarge a drawn picture and it still looks smooth.

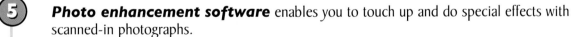

5 **Photo enhancement software** enables you to touch up and do special effects with scanned-in photographs.

6 With *modeling programs*, you can design a three-dimensional object or scene.

7 You can then have the computer figure out what your design looks like from a certain angle.

 Moving pictures
Most modeling programs and some other art programs have animation capabilities, enabling you to make short videos.

 End Task

Designing with the PC

Programs are available to help you design everything from business cards to jet planes. *Desktop publishing software* helps you design and produce newsletters, brochures, and other publications. You can use *presentation software* to design slide shows and other graphics presentations. Other computer design programs help you design crossword puzzles, needlepoint patterns, or building blueprints.

Task 6: Using Desktop Publishing and Other Design Programs

To create a newsletter, brochure, or other publication, create pictures in your graphics program and text in your word processor.

Then combine them using **desktop publishing** software.

Special design programs, such as calendar creators and crossword compilers, are available for specific types of finished publications.

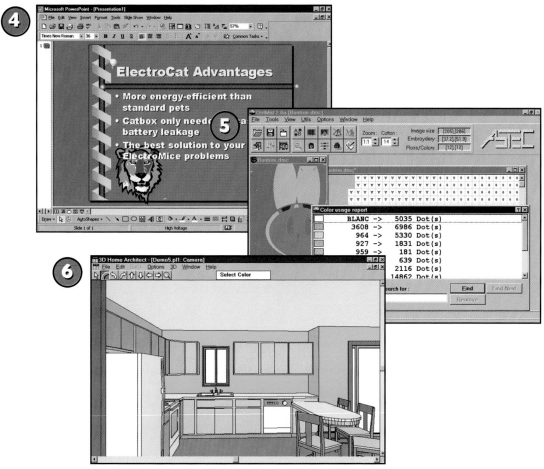

(4) **Presentation software** helps you design sales presentations that you can print on paper, put on an overhead projector, or just show on the computer.

(5) This DotMat cross-stitch program enables you to turn your own drawings into cross-stitch plans.

(6) Some computer architectural design programs let you create and walk through a 3D image of your home design.

✓ **Some popular computer design programs**
Microsoft Publisher and Adobe PageMaker are each examples of popular desktop publishing software. Microsoft PowerPoint is a presentation software product that is part of the Office suite.

Task 7: Using Financial Software

Managing Your Money

Financial software keeps track of your checking accounts, saving accounts, credit cards, and loans. Deluxe financial software can also keep track of your investments in the stock market.

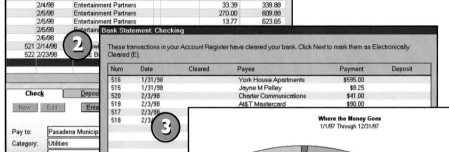

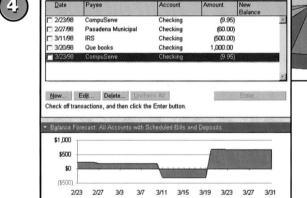

✓ **Popular financial software**

Both the Intuit Quicken and the Microsoft Money series of financial software products are very popular, with different versions for people with different types of finances.

1. Enter each check that you write, each deposit you make, and every item you charge.

2. Your computer can call your bank's computer to verify what checks have cleared and to arrange transfers.

3. The program keeps track of types of expenditures for budget and tax purposes.

4. You can schedule your regular bills to make sure that you don't forget them. Many financial programs can be set up to pay the bills electronically and inform you of the transfer of funds.

End Task

Task 8: Using Games Software

Start Here

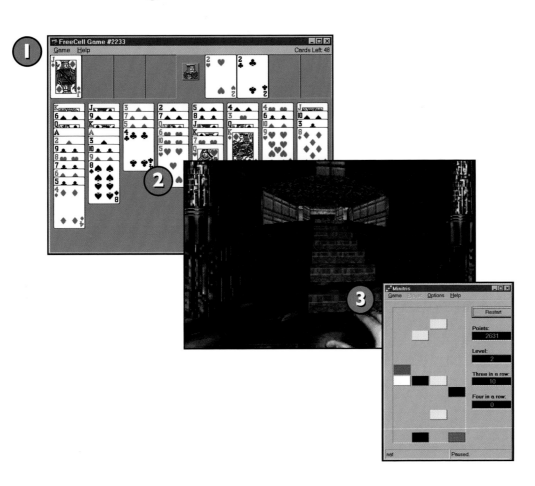

Playing Games on Your PC

Thousands of different games are available for your PC. Some are puzzles or challenges in which you use your wits to get a high score or reach a goal. Other games pit you against an opponent—against someone else using your PC, someone on another computer on the Internet, or even against the computer itself.

✓ **You have some games programs**
Windows 98 comes with some games for your pleasure: Hearts, Minesweeper, and FreeCell are located in the Accessories, Games directory.

✓ **Is your PC good enough?**
Check the system requirements on the game box carefully before you buy it. Many games require a very powerful PC in order to run smoothly.

1 Classic computer games are just traditional board or card games that have been translated into a computer program.

2 Some **simulations** place the player in re-created, real-life scenes and situations, whereas others create fantasy worlds in which the player must compete.

3 **Arcade games** are often very abstract games of skill.

Task 9: Installing Programs

New Programs on Your PC

When you have a new program for your computer, the program not only needs to put files on your hard disk, but also needs information about your PC and about how you want the program set up. The setup program gathers this information and prepares the program and your system to work together.

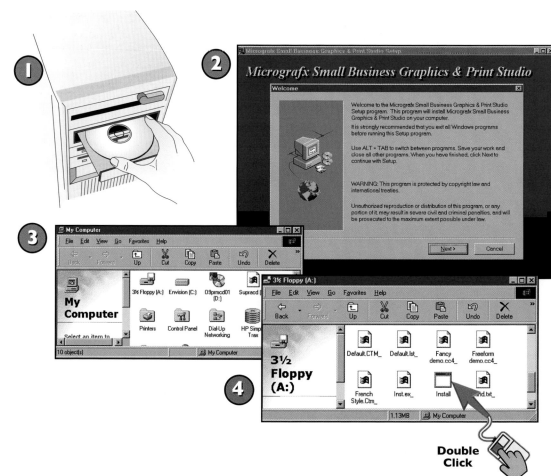

⚠ **WARNING**

To avoid problems, close all open programs before starting any installation.

✓ **Installing downloaded programs**

If you downloaded a program from the Internet, see Part 7, Task 15, for information on installing it.

① Put the program disk into the disk drive.

② If the program is on CD-ROM, wait a few seconds, and you should see the setup program starting. It leads you through the rest of the installation.

③ If the program is on floppy disk, or the installation doesn't start automatically, look at the disk in My Computer (as shown in Part 5, Task 15).

④ Find the icon marked **Setup** or **Install** and double-click it. The installation program starts.

Task 10: Removing Programs

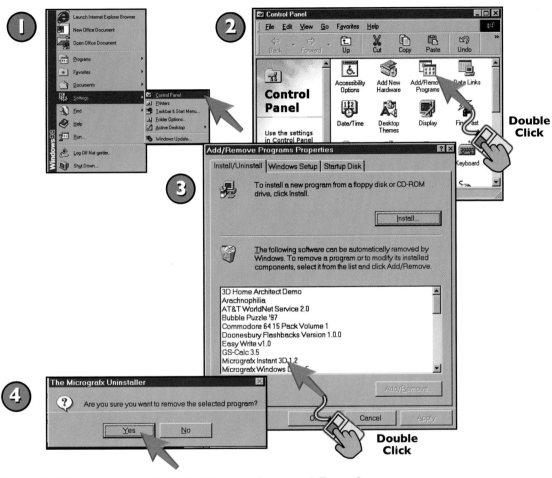

Double Click

Double Click

Uninstalling Old Programs

If you have a program on your PC that you will never use again, you should remove it. Unused programs not only take up important hard disk space, but they slow down your machine.

✔ **Replacing old programs with new** If you're upgrading to a newer version of the same program, you probably won't have to uninstall the old one. The new version takes care of replacing the old files.

✔ **Program not listed?** If the program isn't listed in the Add/Remove Programs list, just locate the program's files on your hard drive and delete them.

1. From the **Start** menu, select **Settings**, **Control Panel**.

2. Double-click the **Add/Remove Programs** icon to open that dialog box.

3. Click the **Install/Uninstall** tab (if it's not on top) and double-click the program name on the list.

4. Choose **Yes**, and the program is removed.

PART 7

Email, the Web, and More

Almost anywhere you go these days, you hear about the Internet, the World Wide Web, and email. This is all about information going from one place to another via computer. It looks like we're not too far from the point where almost as many people have access to computer communications as have access to a telephone. You can use online communications to write to a friend, book a vacation, buy a car, transfer information from your home to your office—the list is endless.

To get online, you need your PC, a modem, and an available phone line. You also need some spare money to pay the monthly bill for the online service or Internet service provider, the companies with powerful computers that your PC passes information through. After you have all that, it's just a matter of installing and setting up some software to get in contact with people, ideas, and services from all over the world. This chapter is your guide to getting connected and to what you can do after you are.

Tasks

Task 1: Understanding Your Modem

What's a Modem?

A *modem* is a device that connects your PC to your telephone line so that your PC can exchange information with other computers. Modem speed is measured in how many *kilobits* (thousands of *bits*, abbreviated *Kb*) of data it can send or receive each second. Modern standard modems run at 28.8Kb, 33.6Kb, or 56Kb, with higher numbers meaning faster, and thus better, modems. (For information on including a modem in your PC purchase, see Part 2, Task 2. To learn how to connect your modem to the phone line, see Part 2, Task 9.)

✓ Do you have a modem?

If you have an *internal modem* in your PC, you see two telephone jacks on the back of your PC. You might have an *external modem*—a small box with phone jacks connected to your PC.

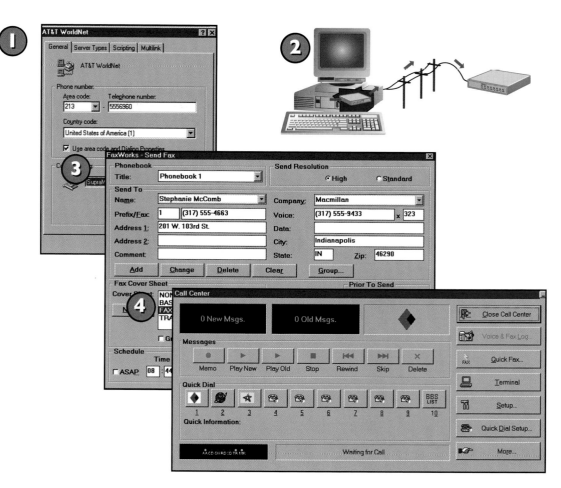

A program tells your modem the number to dial. Another modem answers the call. The two modems figure out which modem is slower (handshaking), and they both talk at that slower speed.

Your PC tells your modem what data to send to the other computer. Your modem then exchanges information with the other modem.

Most modems are **fax modems**, which means they can also be used to receive faxes on your PC and to send PC documents out as faxes.

Voice/fax modems enable your PC to work like an answering machine. Of course, your PC must be left on for this to work.

Task 2: Sending a Fax

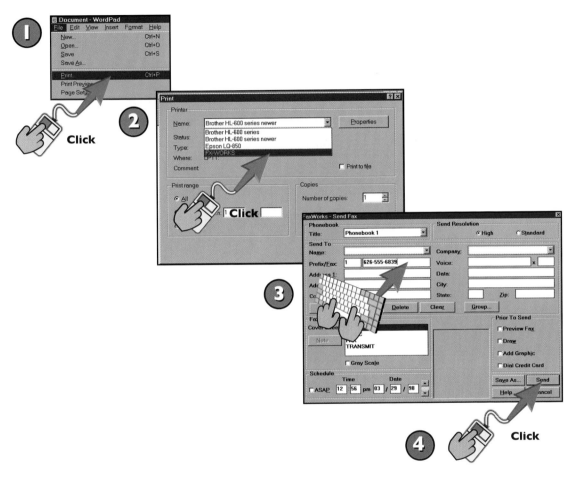

Click

Click

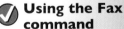

Click

Using Your Fax Modem

If you have a fax modem, you can fax documents directly from your computer to a fax machine. This saves you the trouble of printing the document and taking it to a fax machine (if you even have one). Additionally, the fax that the other person receives looks sharper than if you had faxed it normally. To take advantage of your fax modem, you need to install the fax software that came with the modem. If the modem came already installed in your PC, the software is probably already installed as well. If not, see Part 6, Task 9.

✓ **Using the Fax command**
Some programs have the command **File, Send To, Fax Recipient**, which is a better way to send a fax from that program.

1 With the document that you want to fax open, choose **File, Print**. (Don't use the Print button, which in some programs automatically prints the document.)

2 From the **Name** drop-down menu in the Print dialog box, select the name of your fax program, and click **OK**.

3 The fax program opens a dialog box. Type the phone number for the receiving fax machine into the fax number field.

4 Click the **Send** button (or, if your fax program doesn't have a Send button, the **OK** button), and the fax is sent.

Task 3: Using Online Services

What's an Online Service?

An *online service* is a system to which you can hook up by modem, which gives you access to email, discussions, downloads, online chats, and other features. Although you can get all these things from the World Wide Web, they are more controlled on an online service, and they are not likely to slow down the way that the Web does. These online services also give you access to the Internet.

Start Here

Popular online services

The most popular online services include America Online, CompuServe, and The Microsoft Network.

1 Each online service uses its own custom program to enable you to access it.

2 *Discussion forums* are places for online discussions. Each forum has discussions on a certain topic, such as comics or knitting. Any user of the service can participate.

3 *Chat rooms* enable you to exchange messages quickly with a whole group of members of the online service.

4 Email reaches other members of the online service in minutes, rather than the hours it can take on the Internet.

End Task

Task 4: Understanding the Internet

Start Here

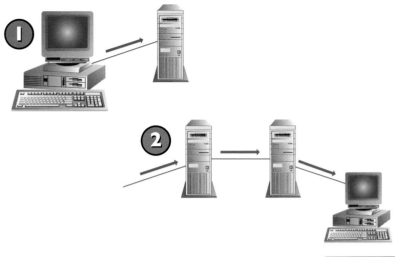

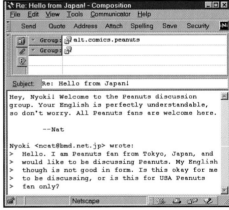

What Is the Internet?

The *Internet* is a network of thousands of computers all over the world, set up to relay information across the globe. To connect to the Internet, you need to pay an *Internet service provider* (*ISP*). The ISP feeds messages to and from your computer into this network, so you can use the Internet to communicate with others online.

✓ **Online services are ISPs**
When you sign up with an online service, it gives you access to the Internet in addition to its own private services.

✓ **Nobody owns the Internet**
The Internet is held together by a bunch of computer owners agreeing to work together. No one company owns or controls it.

① Your Internet messages go from your PC to your *Internet service provider* (*ISP*), the folks who provide your access to the Internet.

② The ISP's computer reads the address of the message, figures out a path through other ISP computers to the right computer, and passes it along.

③ Unlike an online service, which requires membership to use the features of the service, most things on the Internet can be used by anyone, no membership required.

End Task

Task 5: Setting Up for the Internet

Getting Hooked Up

To use the Internet, you have to connect your modem to your phone line, and you must have an account with an Internet service provider (ISP). The ISP connects your computer to the Internet and sets up an email address for you. Windows 98 comes with the Internet Connection wizard, a program to help you find an ISP and to set up your machine to contact its computers.

✓ **Consider a second phone line**
That way, you could still get phone calls while you're on the Internet.

✓ **Not for Windows 95**
Windows 95 has a different Internet Connection wizard, one that assumes that you've already contacted an ISP and gotten the important setup information from it.

Start Here

ChargeMaster

Horatio Spacebunny
5555 4444 3333 2222
Exp 11/03

Click

(1) Hook up your modem to your phone line, as shown in Part 2, Task 9.

(2) Make sure you have your credit card available. The ISP charges the price of your Internet account to your credit card.

(3) Click the **Start** button and choose **Programs**, **Accessories**, **Communications**, **Internet Connection Wizard**.

Next Step

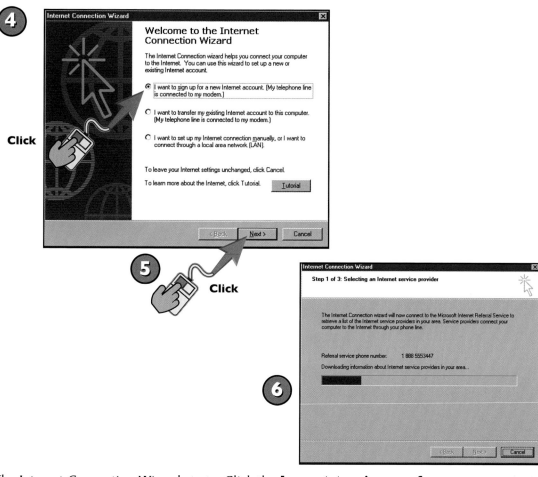

Click

Click

4 The Internet Connection Wizard starts. Click the **I want to sign up for a new Internet account** option button.

5 Click **Next**.

6 The Internet Connection Wizard uses your modem to call a computer at Microsoft and get information about ISPs in your area. Continue to the next task.

Pick Your ISP

Microsoft has deals with a number of ISPs, which makes connecting to those ISPs particularly easy. The Internet Connection Wizard will tell you about the deals that various ISPs offer, and let you select which one you want. Remember, however, that there is more to finding a good ISP than picking the best price. Talk to your friends about what ISPs they use and their experiences with them.

Task 6: Picking an Internet Service Provider

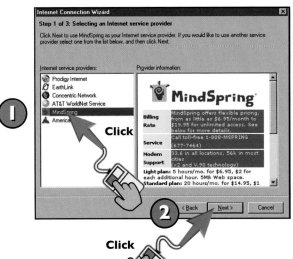

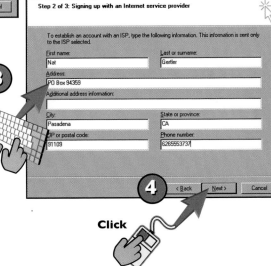

Click

Click

Click

(✓) **Want a different ISP?**
You don't need to limit yourself to the ISPs that Microsoft offers. Any ISP you sign up with will give you the information needed to set up your PC to deal with them.

① Click on the name of an ISP, and information about the ISP and its costs appear. Check each of the ISPs until you find the one you want.

② With the ISP you want displayed, click **Next**.

③ Enter your name, address, and phone number.

④ Click **Next**. Continue to the next task.

Task 7: Choosing a Price Plan

Start Here

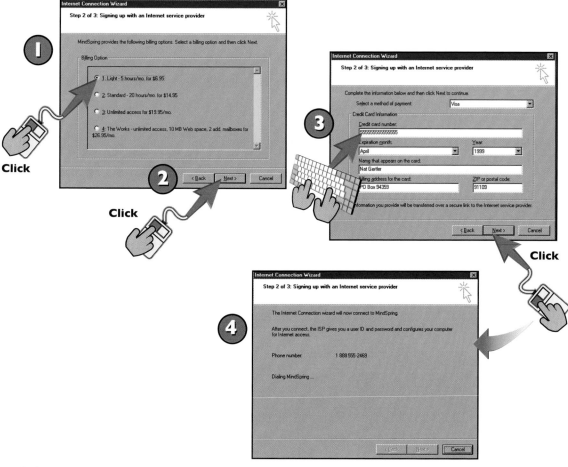

Click

Click

Click

Costs and Billing

ISP deals fall into one of two types. One type lets you connect to the Internet for as long as you want, as often as you want, for one fixed monthly price. Another type charges you a lower price that only covers so many hours of Internet use per month. If you use more than that alotted time, there is an additional charge per hour. It doesn't take a lot of additional use for this rate to actually cost you more than the all-you-can-use rate.

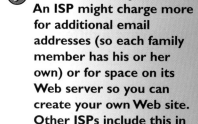

✓ **Added cost options**
An ISP might charge more for additional email addresses (so each family member has his or her own) or for space on its Web server so you can create your own Web site. Other ISPs include this in the price.

① Click on the payment plan you want.

② Click **Next**.

③ Enter your credit card information. Click **Next**.

④ The wizard dials up the ISP and gives its computer your information. Continue to the next task.

End Task

Task 8: Setting Up Your ISP

Finishing the Setup

When your PC sends your billing information to the ISP, the ISP's computer responds by asking for some additional information. The Internet Connection Wizard asks you for some information that is stored on your PC, which will be used whenever you connect to the Internet. The exact set of information used varies from ISP to ISP; what you see in this task is just the example from one ISP. Whatever the wizard asks you, just fill in the answers and click **Next**.

Start Here

Click

Click

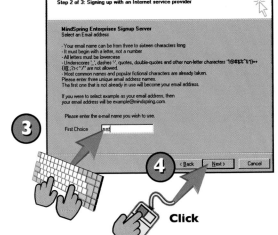

Click

✓ **Checking the phone number**
The front of your white pages has a guide to what phone numbers are in your local (free) calling area.

1 Select a phone number from the list. Make sure it's a number in your local calling area. Otherwise, your Internet connection is a toll call.

2 Click **Next**.

3 Pick a user ID. This is part of your email address, so use your name or something recognizable.

4 Click **Next**.

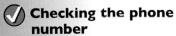 Next Step

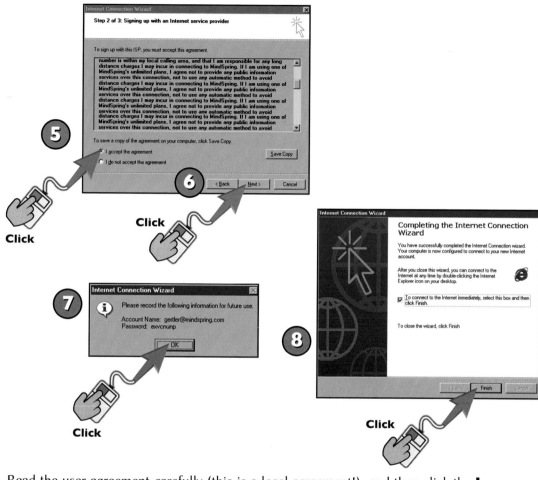

5 Read the user agreement carefully (this is a legal agreement!), and then click the **I accept the agreement** option.

6 Click **Next**.

7 Copy your email address and password, and store them where you won't lose them. Click **OK**.

8 Congratulations, you're set up for the Internet! Click **Finish**.

The World Wide Web

The *World Wide Web* (abbreviated *WWW* or simply the *Web*) is a set of documents (called *Web pages*, grouped together into *Web sites*) spread across computers all over the world and transmitted via the Internet. Using a *Web browser* (a program that enables you to ask for and view Web pages), you can look up information, read stories, play games, and many other things via the Web.

✓ **Not everything is the Web**

Many people use the terms Web and Internet interchangeably. Actually, email and newsgroups are not part of the Web.

✓ **Powerful Web browsers**

Modern Web browsers include Internet Explorer, Netscape Navigator, Netscape Communicator, and Opera.

Task 9: Understanding the World Wide Web

Start Here

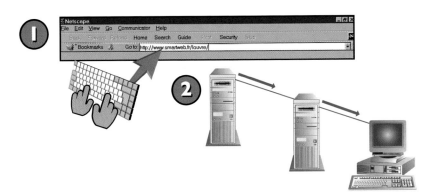

1 When you indicate to the Web browser what Web page you want (such as by typing the page's address), a request for that page is sent out over the modem.

2 The computer that has that page (called a **Web server**) sends it to your PC. The Web browser displays the page text.

3 Text loads first, and pictures take longer to display. If you don't want or need to wait for the pictures on Web pages, you can set your browser options to load just the text.

4 The fully loaded Web page shows pictures, text, and **hyperlinks** (graphics or highlighted text that you can click to move to another Web page or site).

End Task

Task 10: Understanding Web Addresses

http://www.mcp.com/resources/prodapps/ frame_off97.html

1 http://

2 www.mcp.com

3 /resources/prodapps/

4 frame_off97.html

1 The header **http://** means that what follows is a Web address.

2 The **domain name** shows what business or organization's Web site has this page. (Your ISP's computer has a list of what computer stores each Web site.)

3 The **path** shows in what folder (or series of folders) the host computer stores this Web page.

4 The last part is the actual filename of the Web page.

www.Whatever

Web addresses (called *uniform resource locators* or *URLs*) have started showing up on TV shows, soda cans, racecars, and seemingly everywhere else. Your browser uses these addresses to find specific Web pages. When you understand the makeup of a URL, it can provide information for you about a site and its host before you ever visit the site.

✓ **This URL doesn't have a filename!** Sometimes Web addresses include only a *domain name* or only a domain and *path*. Those URLs take you to the Web site's home page.

✓ **What is .com?** In a domain name, .com means a commercial (business) Web site. Government sites have .gov, school sites have .edu, and non-U.S. countries have their own endings (such as .jp for Japan).

End Task

Moving from Web Page to Web Page

Browsing the Web involves moving from site to site, following links, searching for and finding new sources of information and entertainment. Although each Web browser is different, they all involve the same basic processes.

✓ **The Pointing Hand cursor**
Your cursor turns into the shape of a pointing hand when it rests on a link.

✓ **Finding interesting Web pages**
Web directories help you find pages on whatever topic you want. Popular directories include

`http://www.yahoo.com`

`http://www.excite.com`

`http://www.infoseek.com`

Task 11: Browsing the Web

Click

Click

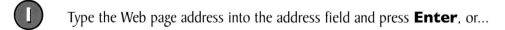

1. Type the Web page address into the address field and press **Enter**, or...

2. ...click a **link**, either underlined text or a picture, which takes you to a page related to that text or picture, or...

3. ...select a favorite page from your **Bookmarks** or **Favorites** menu.

End Task

Task 12: Using Newsgroups

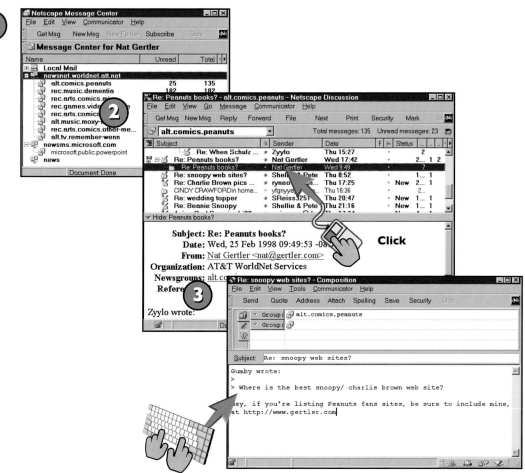

Click

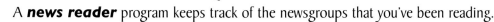

I A **_news reader_** program keeps track of the newsgroups that you've been reading.

I A **_news reader_** program keeps track of the newsgroups that you've been reading.

2 Your news reader displays the message threads and enables you to select one to read.

3 Give your own message a title, enter the text, and use the **Send** command to post it on the newsgroup.

What Is a Newsgroup?

A _newsgroup_ is a discussion forum carried on the Internet. People from all over the world can respond to other people's messages or even start new discussions (_threads_) within the forum. You find newsgroups focusing on everything from comic books to calculus.

✓ Quote the original message
When responding to a message, quote the parts to which you're responding. That way, people who didn't see the first message can follow the conversation. (Many newsreaders automatically quote the entire content of any message to which you reply.)

✓ Find interesting newsgroups
The Web site www.deja.com can help you find newsgroups of interest to you.

Task 13: Sending and Receiving Email

What Is Email?

Email is electronic mail, messages that you can send directly to anyone on the Internet. These messages can include files in addition to text, which means that you can send people pictures, programs, and all sorts of documents.

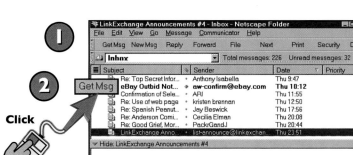

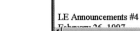

Click

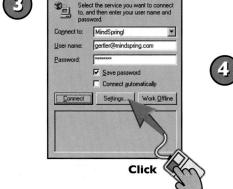

Click

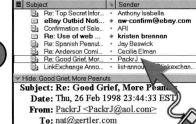

Click

✅ **Email addresses**
The part of the email address before the @ is the person's username on the system. The part after the @ is the domain name of the system that handles the email.

1 Start your email program.

2 Tell the program to get your email (many programs do this automatically).

3 If the Dial-up Connection dialog box appears, click **Connect**. (You can skip this step in the future if you check the **Connect automatically** checkbox now.)

4 Click an email on the list to read it.

Next
Step

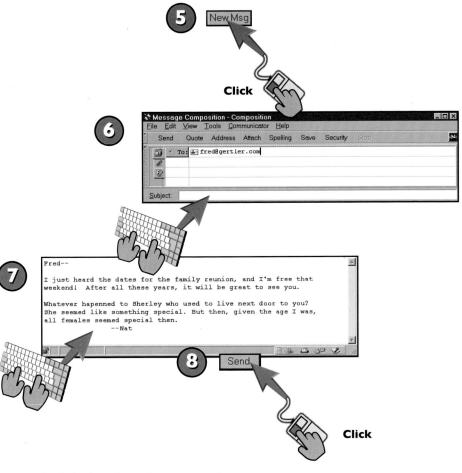

Click

Click

⑤ To write an email, click the **New Message** button.

⑥ Enter the email address for the person to whom you're sending it, and enter a title for the message.

⑦ Type your message.

⑧ While still connected to the Internet, choose **Send**. (If the dialog box from step 3 appears, click **Connect**.) Your message is delivered.

 **Responding to an email?**
Use the Reply command, and your program automatically includes the right email address and subject header.

 End Task

Task 14: Downloading Programs

Software from the Web

There are thousands of programs you can *download* (copy from the Internet to your computer). Some are *freeware* (free software), while others are *shareware* (try it for free, and pay for it only if you keep using it).

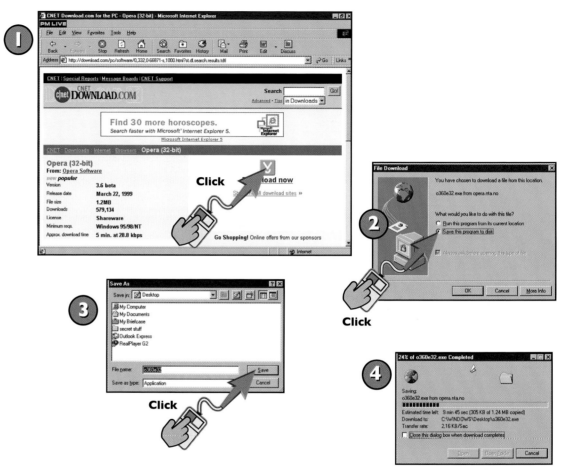

1. Click the download link for the program.

2. If you're asked whether to run the program or save the program to disk, choose the **Save** option and then click **OK**.

3. Use the file dialog box to pick a disk location to store the file (as described in Part 5, Task 8).

4. A download dialog box appears, to show you how the download has progressed.

Task 15: Installing Downloaded Programs

Start Here

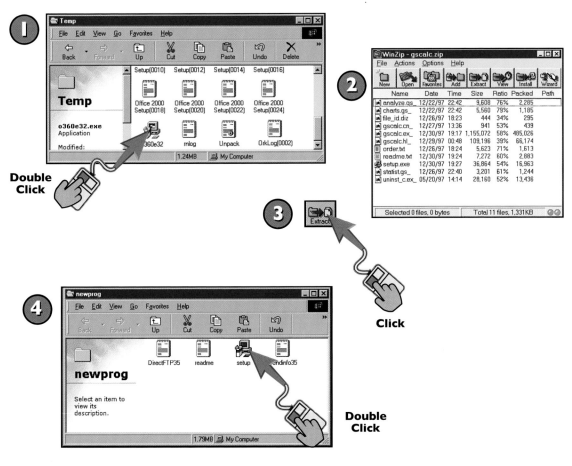

Double Click

Click

Double Click

Different Installation

To make programs easily downloadable, software distributors combine all of a program's files into a single file. Sometimes this file is an executable program file (these end in .exe and when you click an executable file, the program runs). Other times, you download a *zipped file* (ending in .zip). A zipped file contains a number of compressed files, which you must unzip with a special program, such as WinZip or PKZip, before you can run the program.

✅ **Places to get zip programs**
www.winzip.com
www.pkware.com

⚠ **WARNING**
Destructive programs created by would-be saboteurs are often disguised as useful programs. Download only from trusted sources.

① Note the filename while downloading. If the filename ends with .exe, find the icon for the file and double-click it (see Part 5, Task 17).

② If the filename ends with .zip, open it in your zip program.

③ Use the extract command, which enables you to create a new folder and then copies the individual files into the folder.

④ Start the setup program using the file browser (see Part 5, Task 17).

End Task

Task 16: Putting Up Your Own Web Site

A Web Site for You

Creating your own Web site requires a bit of learning and effort, but it's probably the easiest way to put information where millions of people can see it if they want. It's also cheaper than hiring someone to put your site together for you.

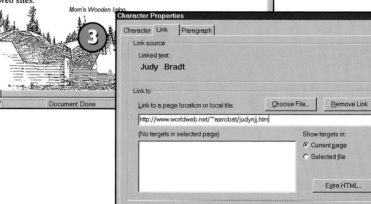

✓ **Buying a domain name**
You can buy a domain name such as **www.gertler.com** for your site. Your ISP hosts your domain name (and charges you for the service). A well-chosen domain name makes it easier for people to remember where your site is.

① Write the text for your Web pages, using a Web page design program (such as Hot Dog or the ones built into versions of Internet Explorer and Netscape Communicator).

② Create or find pictures and add them to your pages.

③ Add links to your pages so that the pages all link to each other.

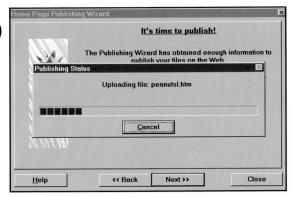

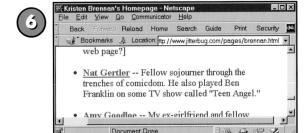

4 Get some space on a Web server. (Your ISP probably offers some space as part of the deal, or you can make a separate deal for some.)

5 Use an ***uploading program*** (usually included with, or built into, the design program) to copy the files from your PC to the Web server.

6 Publicize your site. Start spreading the URL around, and get other people to put links to your site on their sites.

✅ **Handy Web design**
Any word processor with a
Save As HTML command
can be used as a simple
Web design program.

End
Task

PART 8

Taking Care of Your PC

A PC is a machine with literally millions of microscopic parts. If any one of those pieces breaks down, it can cause your computer not to work correctly. In some cases, it can destroy your files, quickly wiping out hundreds of hours of your work. The good news is that PCs don't break down very easily. They're quite easy to take care of, and with a little planning you can make sure that if the worst happens, it's just an irritation rather than a disaster.

Tasks

Task 1: Starting the Backup Program

Why Back Up?

Backing up your files means creating a copy of them that is not stored on your hard disk. If your hard disk breaks down or you accidentally erase an important file, you can recover it from the *backup* (the copy of the files). To back up your files, you need a large removable storage device as described in Part 1, Task 16, such as a tape drive or a Zip drive. You also need blank tapes or disks for that drive. (If you only have a floppy drive, you can use the Copy command shown in Part 5, Task 20, to copy your most important documents onto floppy disks.)

⚠️ **WARNING**
Don't store all your backups near your PC. Keep at least one full backup somewhere else. That way, if the worst happens (a fire, for example), you still have a copy of your files.

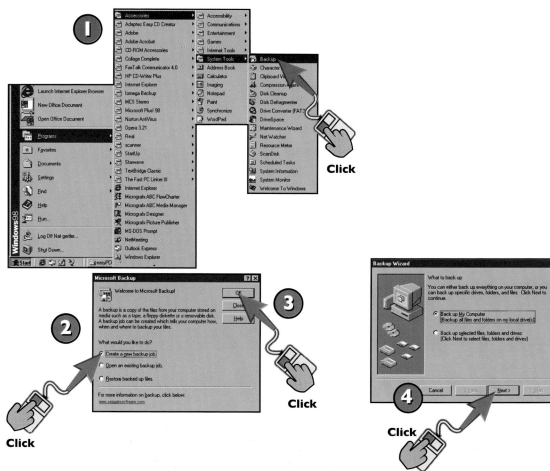

Click

Click

Click

Click

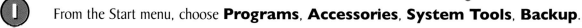

(1) From the Start menu, choose **Programs**, **Accessories**, **System Tools**, **Backup**.

(2) Choose **Create a new backup job** to indicate that you want to back up your disk.

(3) Click **OK**.

(4) The program asks if you want to back up the entire disk or just selected files. Click **Next** to tell it you want the whole disk.

Task 2: Choosing a Full or Incremental Backup

Start Here

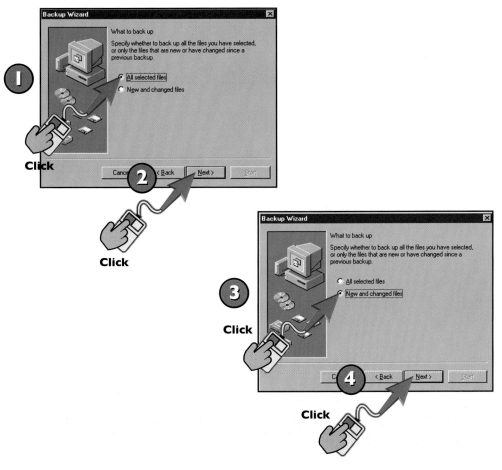

Click

Click

Click

Click

What's the Difference?

A *full backup* is a copy of all of the files on your hard disk. An *incremental backup* only has the files that have changed since the last time you did a full backup. Because it has fewer files, an incremental backup is quicker to make. Using your most recent full backup and most recent incremental backup together, you can get back any file.

1 To do a full backup, select the **All selected files** option.

2 Click **Next**.

3 To do an incremental backup, select the **New and changed files** option.

4 Click **Next**.

 Do some full backups
The longer it has been since your last full backup, the longer the incremental backup will take. About every fifth backup should be a full backup.

End Task

Page 167

Backing Up

Once you've started the backup program (Task 1) and selected a full or partial backup (Task 2), you're ready to actually copy the files.

✓ What to back up onto

Tape drives are popular for backups because you can store several gigabytes on a reusable $20 tape. CD-R and CD-Rewritable drives are also good for backups (see Part 1 of this book for more information on those drives).

⚠ WARNING

Not all drives work with Microsoft Backup software. You might need to use special software that came with your tape drive. Your CD-R or CD-Rewritable drive might have special software needed to prepare the disk before using Backup.

Task 3: Backing Up Your Files

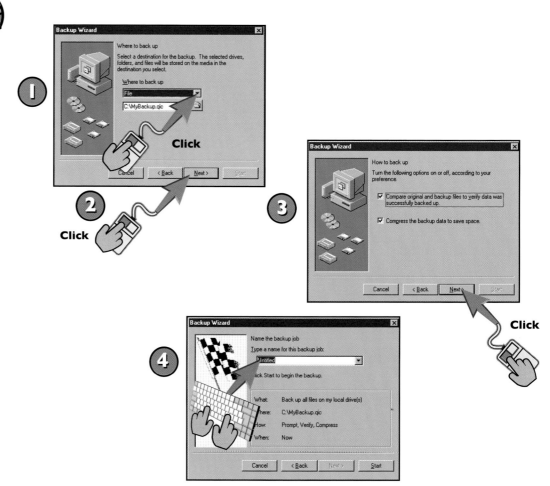

Select your tape drive from the list. To back up to a disk, select **File**, click the folder button, then select that disk drive using the file browser that appears.

Click **Next**.

Click **Next** again.

Type a name for this backup, then click **Start**. The backup begins.

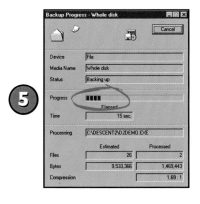

Click

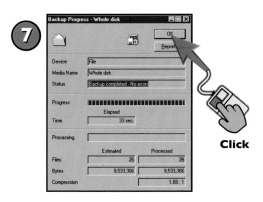

Click

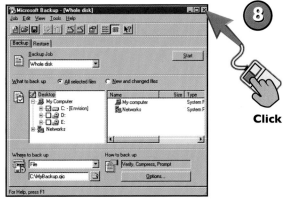

Click

Click

⑤ A progress meter shows you how much of the backup is complete. Backups often take hours to complete. If you fill a tape or disk, you will be asked to insert another one.

⑥ When the backup is complete, this dialog box appears. Click **OK**.

⑦ Click **OK** to remove the backup progress dialog box.

⑧ Click the **Close** button to close the backup program.

End Task

Task 4: Restoring a Backed Up File

Copying the Files Back

If disaster strikes and you lose a file, you can use the Backup program to recover the file (if, of course, you previously backed it up). The program is smart enough that it won't restore the file if it finds you have a version on the hard disk.

✓ **Restore entire folders**
In step 6, check a folder check box to restore the whole folder, or the hard disk's check box to restore the entire disk.

✓ **Completely restoring**
If you've lost all your files, first restore from the most recent full backup. If you have an incremental backup that's newer than the full backup, restore that next.

Start Here

Click

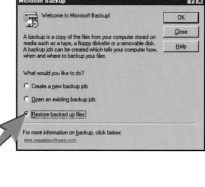

Click

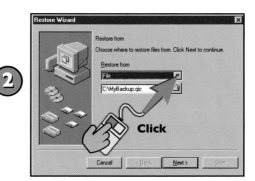

Click

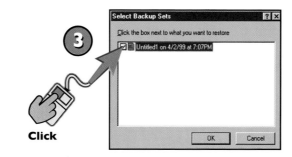

Click

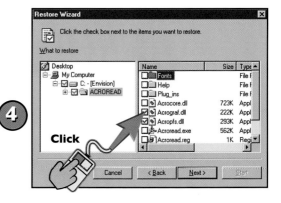

Click

① Start Microsoft Backup (see Task 1, step 1). Click the **Restore backed up files** option, then click **OK**.

② Select your tape drive. If restoring from a disk, select **File**, click the folder icon, then use the file browser to select the backup file you created. Click **Next**.

③ Check the box next to the backup that contains the file you want to restore, then click **OK**.

④ Double-click disk and folder names to see what was backed up from those disks and folders. Check the check box next to files you want to restore. Click **Next** when done.

Next Step

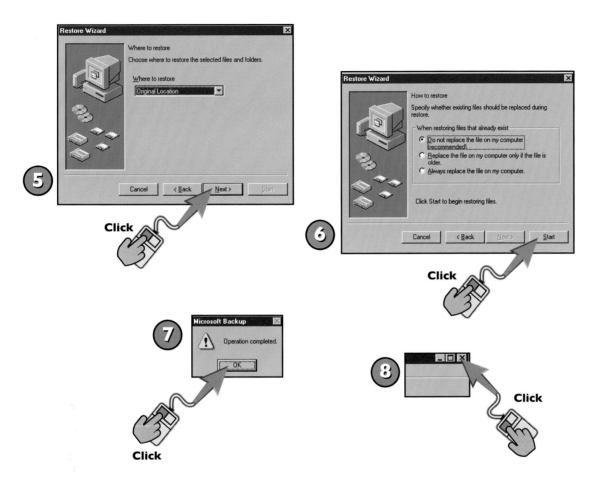

5   Click **Next**.

6   Click **Start**. The program now finds the files you want from within the backup file, and restores your files to your hard disk.

7   When the backup is complete, the system lets you know. Click **OK** on the dialog box, and again on the Restore Progress dialog box.

8   Click the **Close** button to leave the backup program.

Task 5: Checking for Hard Disk Errors

Problems with Your Hard Disk

Hard disk problems are of two main kinds—the scrambling of information on the disk, so the system loses all or part of some files, and physical damage to an area of the disk. If you're running Windows 98, the operating system automatically checks for damage if you leave the PC on overnight on Wednesday. If you're using Windows 95, this task shows you how to do a Standard check (checking for the first type of errors) or a Thorough check (which takes longer, but checks for both types.

When to run ScanDisk

Use this task if you're having trouble getting a program to start, if a program indicates that it's having trouble reading files, if files are missing, or if a document has strange content that you had not entered.

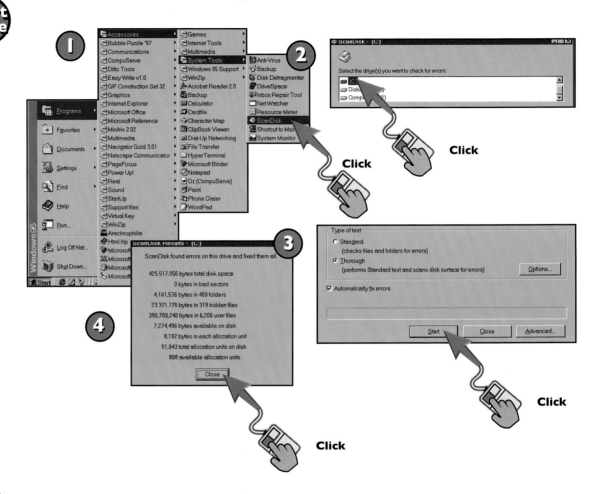

Click

Click

Click

Click

Click

1. For Windows 95 users, from the **Start** menu, choose **Programs**, **Accessories**, **System Tools**, **ScanDisk**.

2. Click the name of the hard disk that you want to check.

3. Choose a check type (**Thorough** or **Standard**) and then choose **Start**. The program starts the check.

4. When it's finished, ScanDisk reports the results. Click **Close**.

End Task

Task 6: Speeding Up Your Hard Disk

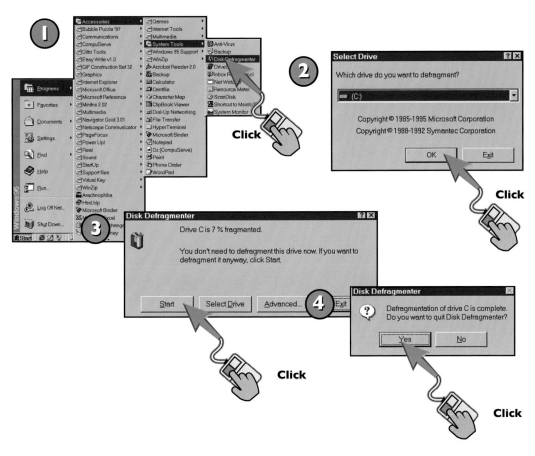

Click

Click

Click

Click

Defragmenting

If you've ever shared a Sunday newspaper, you know that you can end up with pieces of the paper in various piles, making it hard to find the section you're looking for. A hard disk is like that. Over time, pieces of files get spread all over the place, and it takes longer for the computer to find the pieces that it needs. *Defragmenting* **your hard disk puts the pieces back in order. Windows 95 users should use this task periodically, but only after running ScanDisk to check for disk errors. (Windows 98 defragments automatically if you leave the PC on Thursday night.)**

⊘ WARNING

Keep all programs closed while running the disk defragmenter, and don't start any more until it's finished. Also, because defragmenting can take hours, it's best to do it when you won't need to use the PC for a while, such as at night.

1. Windows 95 users: After running ScanDisk (see Task 5), from the **Start** menu, choose **Programs**, **Accessories**, **System Tools**, **Disk Defragmenter**.

2. In the Select Drive dialog box, select the disk (or disks, if you have more than one hard drive) that you want to defragment and choose **OK**.

3. Choose **Start**, and the program begins. Depending on the size, speed, and degree of disorganization, the defragmentation could take several hours.

4. When finished, click **Yes**.

Task 7: Cleaning Your Mouse

Dirt in the Mouse

When dust and dirt get into your mouse, moving the mouse smoothly becomes difficult, and it's tough to move the pointer to a specific spot onscreen. If your pointer is skipping around erratically on the screen, you may be able to solve the problem by cleaning the mouse.

Start Here

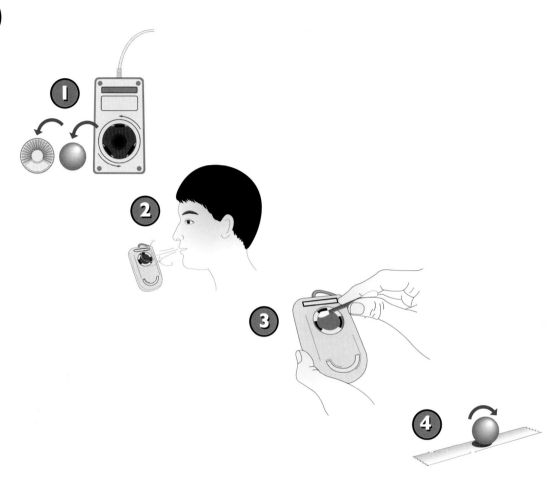

⚠ WARNING
Clean your mouse while your computer is off so that you don't accidentally give the system commands.

✓ No ball?
Optical mice have no ball and don't need cleaning. If the pointer doesn't move smoothly, clean your mouse pad.

① Take the ball cover off the bottom of your mouse. An arrow on the cover indicates how to push or twist the cover.

② Blow dust out of the ball hole.

③ Clean the rollers in the hole using a cotton swab dampened with isopropyl alcohol (rubbing alcohol).

④ Clean the ball by rolling it on adhesive tape, and reassemble the mouse.

End Task

Task 8: Performing Weekly Maintenance

Start Here

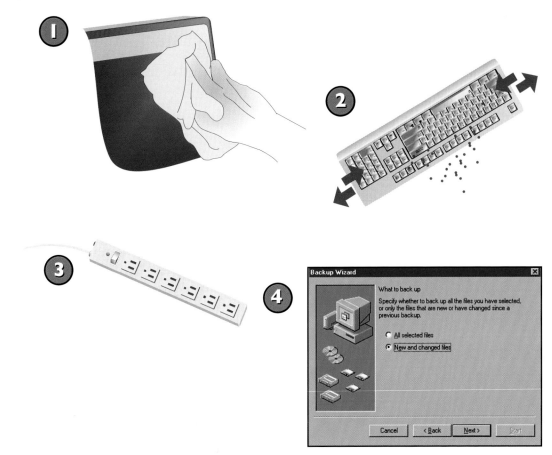

Once-a-Week Procedure

Every week, you should do some simple maintenance things to keep your system working well. These help ensure that your monitor picture doesn't start looking funny, that your system runs smoothly, and that you don't lose your files.

1. With a clean soft rag, wipe the dust from your PC, monitor, and peripherals.

2. Turn your keyboard upside down and shake it gently to dislodge accumulated dust and crumbs.

3. Check the little light on the surge protector (probably marked protection or safe). If it's off or flickering, it's time for a new surge protector.

4. Do an incremental backup (see Tasks 1 through 3 to learn how to do a backup).

 Keep it the same day
Pick a day of the week when you always do your weekly checkup, and do it before doing anything else with your PC so that you don't forget.

 End Task

Page
175

Task 9: Performing Monthly Maintenance

Monthly Procedure

Some maintenance tasks are too time-consuming to do every week, and they really don't need to be done frequently. Don't use that as an excuse, however, not to do them at all.

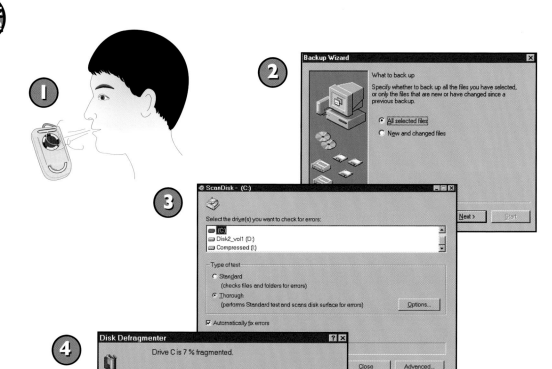

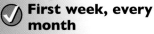

First week, every month

Do your monthly maintenance with the first weekly maintenance procedure every month. Because you're doing a full backup, you don't need to do the incremental backup that week.

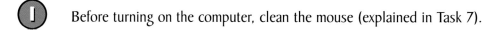

1 Before turning on the computer, clean the mouse (explained in Task 7).

2 Turn on the computer and do a full backup (see Tasks 1 through 3 to learn how to do a backup).

3 Run ScanDisk to check the disk for errors (explained in Task 5; Windows 98 users should just leave their PCs running overnight on Wednesday).

4 Defragment your hard disk (explained in Task 6; Windows 98 users should leave their PCs running overnight on Thursday).

Task 10: Restarting Windows

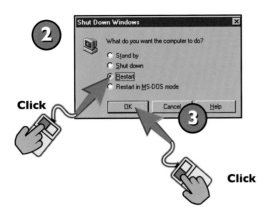

Click

Click

Click

Why Restart?

Sometimes, when you install a program, the setup program prompts you to restart Windows. That's because the installation changes a file that Windows checks when it starts up, and it needs Windows to check that file before it can run. Also, when Windows slows down or starts acting oddly, restarting Windows can clear up the problem. Restarting is also known as rebooting.

WARNING

To avoid losing any information, close all programs before restarting.

Faster restart

When restarting after an installation, hold down **Shift** during steps 2 and 3. (Don't do this if you're restarting because Windows is acting strangely.)

1 From the **Start** menu, choose **Shut Down**.

2 Choose **Restart** in the Shut Down Windows dialog box.

3 Click **OK**.

4 Windows shuts down and then restarts.

Task 11: Creating a Startup Disk

What's a Startup Disk?

If you have a problem with your hard disk, you may not be able to get your system started, so you won't be able to run the programs to fix your hard disk. That's when you want a startup disk, a floppy disk that holds an operating system and some programs that can help you fix the hard drive problems. If something goes wrong with your system and Windows won't start, put the startup disk in the floppy drive and press the reset button. Your system starts up using the operating system from the startup disk.

✓ **DOS, not Windows**
The startup disk starts the system in DOS (disk operating system), a text-oriented operating system. If you have a problem, you may need someone who knows DOS to help you get Windows working again.

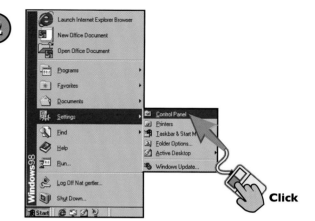

Click

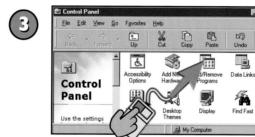

Double
Click

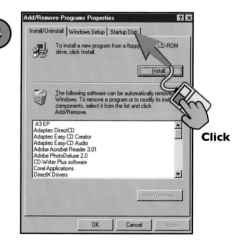

Click

1 Put your Windows CD-ROM in your CD-ROM drive. Press **Shift** while closing the CD-ROM drive, and hold it for ten seconds.

2 From the **Start** menu, choose **Settings**, **Control Panel**.

3 Double-click **Add/Remove Programs**.

4 Click the **Startup Disk** tab in the Add/Remove Programs Properties dialog box.

Next Step

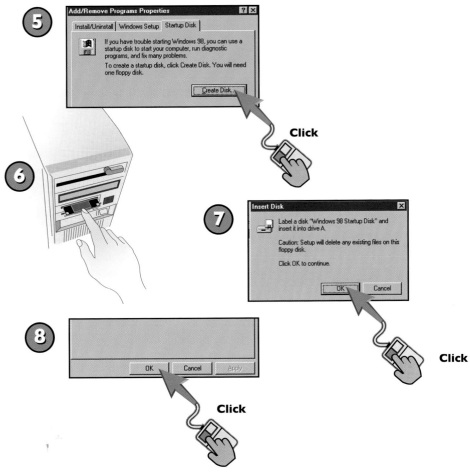

Click

Click

Click

(5) Click **Create Disk**.

(6) Put a blank floppy disk into the floppy drive.

(7) Click **OK**. The Startup disk is made.

(8) Click the **OK** button (it is grayed out until the disk is created and time for you to close the program).

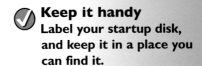 **Keep it handy**
Label your startup disk, and keep it in a place you can find it.

End Task

Task 12: Handling Problems

When Something Goes Wrong

Things do go wrong: Programs don't work right, or hardware breaks down. The most important thing, however, is not to panic. What looks like a completely ruined computer or a loss of weeks of work may take but minutes to fix. The following are some things to try when you run into difficulties, running from what to do in the most mild case to what to do when nothing else works.

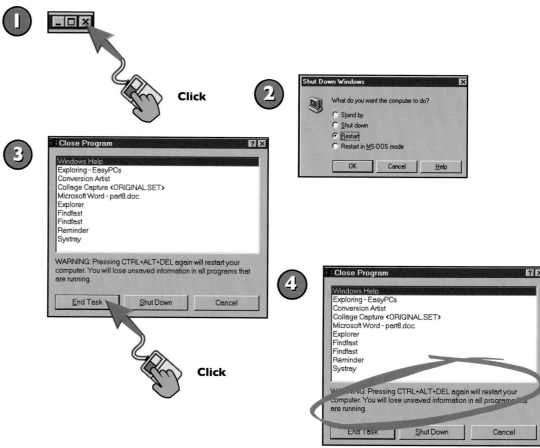

Start Here

Click

Click

✓ **Find out who knows**
You probably have many friends and coworkers who use PCs, and you probably know at least one expert. Find out who that is, and use that person when you get boggled.

1 If a program is working oddly, close it, open it back up, and see whether it works the same.

2 Restart Windows (explained in Task 10), and retry whatever went wrong.

3 If you can't get a program to respond, press **Ctrl+Alt+Delete** and use this dialog box to close it.

4 If closing programs doesn't get Windows working again, select **Ctrl+Alt+ Delete** twice to restart Windows.

Next Step

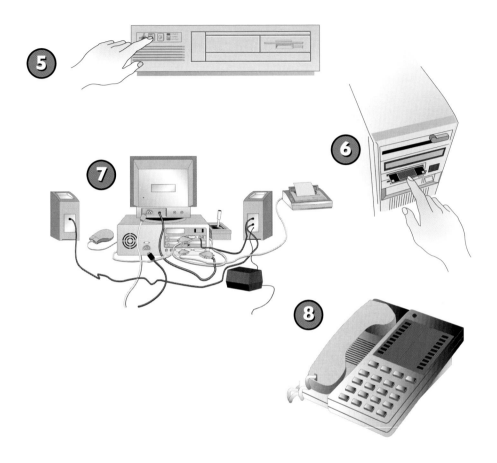

5 If Windows won't restart after step 4, press the reset button on the front of your PC.

6 If Windows won't start up properly, put your boot disk into the floppy drive and then press the reset button. (See Task 11 for more on boot disks.)

7 If your monitor stays black or some other peripheral won't work, check all power switches (including the surge protector) and make sure that the cables are firmly in place.

8 Call the hardware or software manufacturer's technical support hotline.

✓ Finding tech support numbers

The phone numbers and Web addresses for hardware and software tech support are usually in the manuals. Also, software support numbers can be found by selecting Help, About in the program.

Task 13: Solving Printer Problems

Each Printer Is Different

Because of the many different printer models, many variations are possible for changing ink or adding paper. Your printer manual can give you a lot of specific information on printer maintenance. Some general troubleshooting guidelines follow.

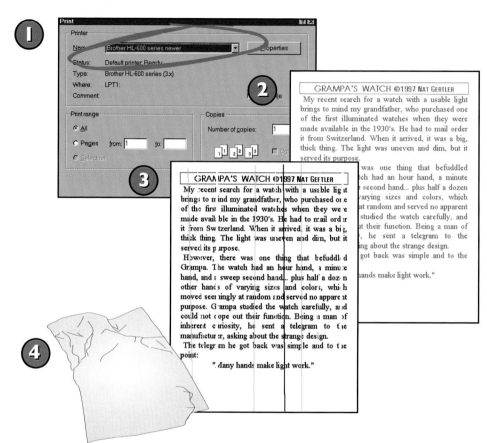

✓ **Inkjets need good paper**
Your printouts look a lot better if you have special inkjet paper.

1. If it doesn't print at all, check the cables and the printer's error lights (you may need to reset the printer). If that doesn't help, choose **File**, **Print** and verify the Name field.

2. Faint printing means that you need more ink or a new toner cartridge.

3. Vertical streaks from a laser printer means that you need to clean the corona wire or get a new printer drum (check your printer's manual for instructions).

4. If the paper crumples or gets stuck in the printer, too much paper is in the bin or a scrap of paper is stuck in your printer's paper path.

Task 14: Saving Electricity

Start Here

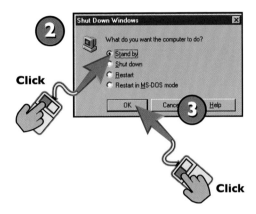

Click

Click

Click

Going into Standby Mode

Most computers sold these days have many energy-saving features. If your PC has them, Windows will automatically set up features which will turn off your hard disk and your monitor if you don't use your PC for a while. If you know you're going to be away from your desk, you can put your PC into standby mode, where the hard disk and screen are turned off, but are ready to come back on quickly when you need them.

1. From the **Start** menu, select **Shut Down**.

2. In the Shut Down Windows dialog box, choose the **Stand by** option.

3. Click **OK**, and your PC will go into standby mode.

4. To awaken your PC out of standby mode, push the on button on the front of your PC.

✓ **A must for laptops**
Laptop PC users should get used to using standby mode. The more energy you save, the longer your battery will last without needing recharging.

End Task

Page
183

Task 15: Understanding Upgrades

Improving Your Computer

You can replace individual PC pieces with newer or better versions, without having to replace the whole PC. You don't need to be a computer scientist to do most of these changes. The easy upgrades are about as hard as hooking the VCR to the TV or changing your car battery. Replacements of medium difficulty are about as hard as hooking up a whole entertainment system or changing your spark plugs. For the harder tasks, you probably want to pay your computer store to do it for you.

✓ **Learning to upgrade**
For medium-difficulty tasks, you may want to use a book, such as *Upgrading PCs Illustrated*, by Jim Boyce (Que, 1997).

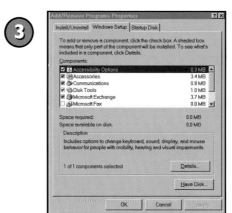

1. Upgrading a program is easy, and is done the same way as a new one (explained in Part 6, Task 9).

2. Changing your printer, monitor, keyboard, or mouse is easy. Unplug the old one, plug in a new one, and install a driver program.

3. Upgrading to a new version of Windows is of medium difficulty.

4. Adding more RAM is of medium difficulty. It's a good, affordable way to speed up your computer.

Next Step

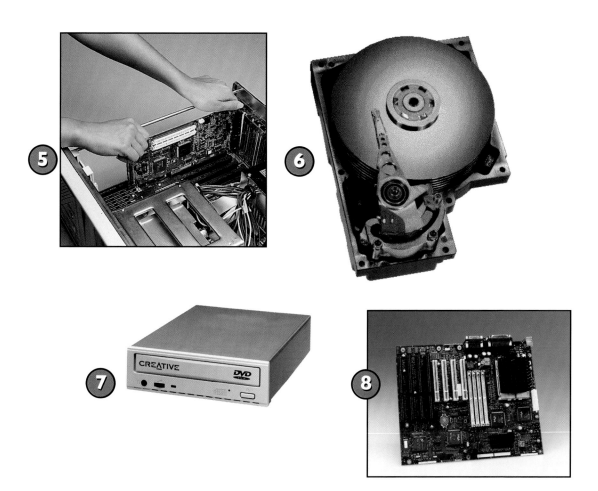

5 Adding a better modem, sound card, or video card is harder than adding RAM, but still not hard.

6 If you're running out of hard disk space, adding a second hard disk is of medium difficulty.

7 Upgrading your CD drive to a CD-R, CD-RW, or DVD drive is of medium difficulty.

8 Replacing your motherboard, your CPU, or your hard disk is hard, because a lot of things can go wrong.

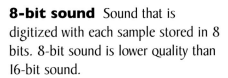
8-bit sound Sound that is digitized with each sample stored in 8 bits. 8-bit sound is lower quality than 16-bit sound.

16-bit operating system A system designed to handle information in groups of 16 bits at a time, in which two bytes of data can be processed simultaneously. Microsoft Windows 3.1 is a 16-bit operating system.

16-bit program A program designed to handle information in groups of 16 bits at a time.

16-bit sound Sound that is digitized with each sample stored in 16 bits. 16-bit sound is higher quality than 8-bit sound.

32-bit operating system An operating system that is designed to handle information in groups of 32 bits at a time and that can process 4 bytes of data simultaneously. Microsoft Windows NT and UNIX are true 32-bit operating systems. Microsoft Windows 95 and 98 can handle 32-bit programs, as well as 16-bit programs.

32-bit program A program designed to handle information in groups of 32 bits at a time.

Alt A combination key that you hold while pressing another key to enter a command.

amplified speakers Speakers with batteries or a power adapter.

applications Programs that help you get work done.

arcade game A computer action game.

ASCII The code used to store text as numbers.

backplate The edge of an expansion card that shows through the back of the PC.

backup To store copies of hard disk files; also, the stored copies.

bit The smallest piece of data, which stores one of two values (zero or one).

boot disk See **startup disk**.

box Scrollbar rectangle that shows what part of a document is displayed.

byte A data storage amount made up of 8 bits, enough to store one of 256 values.

cable modem A device that connects your PC to the Internet via cable TV connections.

CardBus card A special expansion card type for laptops.

cathode ray tube See **CRT**.

CD-R drive (compact disc–recordable) A disc drive that can read and record CD-ROMs.

CD-ROM (compact disc–read-only memory) A compact disc from which the computer can only read information. The computer cannot add to or change data written to a CD-ROM.

CD-RW drive (compact disc–rewritable) A disk drive that can read CD-ROMs and read and write its own CD-RW media.

Celeron A line of processors introduced in 1998 by Intel that can run Windows and both 16-bit and 32-bit programs. The Celeron is designed to be used in low-priced PCs, and processes somewhat slower than a Pentium II running at the same speed. The Celeron is currently available in various models running at speeds ranging from 300 to 433MHz.

cell One space in the grid of a spreadsheet, formed at the intersection of a row and a column.

central processing unit See **CPU**.

chat room An online place where you can exchange messages with someone who is online at the same time.

checkbox A dialog box square used to select or deselect an option.

choose Click an onscreen button or menu option.

click To press and release the left mouse button once rapidly.

close To get rid of a window or shut down a program.

Close button The X button on the right end of a title bar used to close a window or program.

combination keys Keys (such as Ctrl) that you hold down while pressing another key to issue a command.

compact disc (CD) A plastic disc that uses optical storage techniques to store up to 72 minutes of music or 650M of digitally encoded computer data. (*See also* **CD-R drive**, **CD-ROM**, and **CD-RW drive**.)

computer An information processing machine.

context-sensitive A program feature that provides options, menus, documentation, and other controls specific to the command, mode, or action that you are performing.

CPU (central processing unit) The computer's main processing chip.

CRT (cathode ray tube) The monitor.

Ctrl A combination key that you hold while pressing another key in order to give a program command.

cursor An onscreen marker (sometimes called the insertion point) that shows you where in the document your typing will appear.

cycle One beat of the central processing unit's timing clock.

data Information (such as text, numbers, sounds, and images) in a form that can be processed by a computer.

database A file containing a collection of related information that a computer program can manipulate.

database program A program designed to sort and manage lists of information.

defragment To reorganize data on a disk. The more efficient organization makes the disk work faster.

design software Computer programs used to design three-dimensional objects.

desktop The background of the Windows display.

desktop PC A system unit designed to sit lengthwise on a desk.

desktop publishing Designing printed documents on a PC.

dialog box An onscreen message box that conveys information to or requests information from the user.

digital graphics Pictures encoded as numbers.

digital sound Sound encoded as numbers.

digital versatile disc See **DVD**.

DIMM (Dual Inline Memory Module) One type of computer card that holds RAM (random access memory).

discussion forum A place for ongoing online discussions.

disk controller A set of computer chips that manage instructions for the disk drive.

DNS (domain name server) A computer that knows which computer holds the Web pages for each domain name.

domain name Part of a Web address that indicates who owns or manages a Web site. (For example, in the Web address http://www.gertler.com, the domain name is gertler.com.)

domain name server See **DNS**.

dots per inch A measure of the resolution (fineness) of digitized graphics.

double-click To press and release the left mouse button twice rapidly.

download Copy a file from another computer via modem.

drag To move the mouse pointer while holding down a mouse button.

drag-and-drop To move a highlighted onscreen object by dragging it with the mouse and dropping it in a new location by releasing the mouse button.

drag-and-drop editing A program feature that enables you to add items or rearrange items within a document by dragging.

DRAM (Dynamic random access memory) A type of random access memory that periodically refreshes the electrical charge in its capacitors.

draw program A program that enables you to create graphics as a series of lines and shapes.

drive bays Areas in a PC where a drive can be installed.

driver A program that translates computer commands into commands that a specific device understands.

drop Releasing the mouse button at the end of a drag.

drop-down button An onscreen button with a down arrow used to open a drop-down list.

drop-down list An onscreen list of options from which you can select one item.

Dual Inline Memory Module See **DIMM**.

DVD (digital versatile disc) A new CD-like disc used to store data or movies.

EDO RAM (Extended Data Output random access memory) A form of RAM faster than regular RAM.

email Electronic mail; messages sent to people via computer.

Energy Star compliant PC devices designed to save energy.

entertainment PC A PC set up to also act as a TV and stereo.

Esc A keyboard key used to cancel a command or operation.

expansion card A circuit board that fits into a computer's expansion slot and that gives the computer added capabilities, such as enabling it to accept a new sound card or other device.

expansion slot A connector on the motherboard that accepts an expansion card.

Extended Data Output random access memory See **EDO RAM**.

extension A three-letter suffix (such as .DOC, .BMP, or .XLS) added to the end of a filename to describe the file's contents.

external modem A modem with its own case, cables, and power supply, that plugs into a serial port.

F keys See **function keys**.

fax modem A modem that can also send and receive faxes.

female connector A cable connector with holes, not pins.

field A category of information on a database record, such as Name or Date.

file A named storage area on a disk that holds a single set of data.

file browser A window that shows the icons for disk files, letting you find, rename, move, copy, or delete files.

file dialog box A dialog box that enables you to specify an existing file or name a new one.

financial software Programs that manage bank accounts and other finances.

flatbed scanner A scanner in which the document isn't moved while being scanned.

floppy A floppy disk or floppy drive.

floppy disk A removable information storage disk.

floppy drive A device that reads and writes data on floppy disks.

folder A file that holds other files within it.

font A type style.

format To set up a disk for holding data.

freeware Software that you never have to pay for.

full backup The storing of a copy of all your hard disk files.

function keys The keyboard keys marked F1, F2, and so on, used to give programs commands.

GB A gigabyte.

gig A gigabyte.

gigabyte About a billion bytes of data.

grayed out A command or option that is about the same color as the background, indicating that you cannot use it now.

hard disk An internal data storage device installed in your PC.

hardware The physical parts of your PC.

hyperlink A portion of a document or Web page that, when clicked, causes another document or Web page to be displayed.

IBM compatible (International Business Machines compatible) A PC that can run DOS or Windows.

icon A picture that represents a file, drive, or command.

incremental backup A backup that stores only files that have changed since your last full backup.

inkjet printer A printer that prints by squirting ink onto paper.

input Information going into a program.

input device A device such as a keyboard or mouse that is used to give information to a PC.

insertion bar Another name for insertion point.

insertion point An onscreen line that marks where your typing will appear (also referred to as a cursor).

Integrated Services Digital Network See **ISDN**.

internal modem A modem that fits inside your PC.

internal storage device Any device inside your system unit that stores information.

Internet A worldwide network of computers linked to share data.

Internet service provider See **ISP**.

interpolation Increasing the resolution of a scanned image by having a program guess what color each smaller dot would be.

ISA A type of expansion slot used for slower devices.

ISDN (Integrated Services Digital Network) An enhanced phone line available from most local phone companies that enables you to use faster modems designed specifically for such lines.

ISP (Internet service provider) A company that provides Internet accounts and connections to individuals and businesses.

Jaz drive A popular brand of removable hard disk used for storing and transporting large amounts of data.

K See **KB**.

K6 A line of processors introduced by AMD (Advanced Micro Devices, Inc.) in 1996 that can run the Microsoft Windows operating system and both 16-bit and 32-bit programs. The performance of the K6-2 is competitive with the Pentium II running at the same speeds. The performance of the K6-III is competitive with the Pentium III running at the same speeds. The K6 line is currently available in various models running at speeds ranging from 300 to 450 megahertz.

KB (kilobyte) About a thousand bytes.

Kb (kilobit) A measurement used to indicate how many thousands of bits per second a modem can transmit.

keyboard An input device with letter and number keys.

kilobit See **Kb**.

kilobyte See **KB**.

label A spreadsheet cell that holds descriptive text.

LAN (local area network) A system of cables used to connect PCs typically within a single building so that they can share information and devices.

laptop PC A portable one-piece PC, also known as a notebook PC.

laser printer A printer that presses toner onto the paper.

link An area on a Web page that you click to see another page. *See also* **hyperlink**.

local area network *See* **LAN**.

local bus Fast circuitry on the motherboard that connects the CPU to other devices.

LS-120 A type of floppy drive that stores up to 120 megabytes on special disks. (Also called SuperDisk.)

male connector A cable connector with pins rather than holes.

margins The blank space at the edges of a printed page.

Maximize button A button on the title bar that you click to enlarge the window.

MB (megabyte) About a million bytes of data.

meg *See* **MB**.

megabyte *See* **MB**.

menu A clickable list of commands in a single category.

menu bar A bar near the top of a window displaying clickable command categories.

MHz (megahertz) The measurement used to indicate how many cycles a processor has per second.

millisecond *See* **ms**.

Minimize button A button on the title bar that you click to hide the window.

MMX (MultiMedia eXtensions) An enhancement that enables a processor to handle sound and video more quickly than a processor without that enhancement.

modeling program Software that enables you to design a three-dimensional object on your PC and choose an angle from which to view it.

modem A device that enables your PC to communicate with other computers via a phone line.

monitor The PC screen.

motherboard The main board in your system unit.

mouse A hand-held input device designed with one or more buttons on its upper surface and a rolling ball on its underside. Rolling the mouse on a hard surface moves the onscreen pointer in a corresponding direction; clicking a mouse button issues a command to the active operating system or application.

ms (millisecond) A thousandth of a second.

multitasking The capability to run more than one program at a time.

My Computer An icon on your desktop that represents all the files on your system. Double-clicking the My Computer icon opens a file browser so that you can find and work with your files.

nanosecond *See* **ns**.

network PC A PC specifically designed for use when connected to other PCs over a local area network.

news reader A program that enables you to read newsgroup discussions.

newsgroup A discussion group on the Internet.

ns (nanosecond) A billionth of a second.

OCR (Optical Character Recognition) A program that reads text out of a scanned image and inserts it in a document.

online

online Refers to the condition of being connected and able to communicate with a computer. For example, your printer is online when it is ready to receive pages to print from your PC; your PC is online when it is communicating with other computers via the Internet.

online service A company that enables you to connect your PC to its computers via modem so that you can use its chat areas, discussion groups, and email service.

open To start a program, create a window, or display a document or menu.

operating system Your PC's main software (usually Windows), which tells your PC how to manage other programs and all the devices.

Optical Character Recognition See **OCR**.

option button A circle in a dialog box that enables you to select one out of several listed options.

OS See **operating system**.

output The printed or displayed results of processing operations; also

used to describe the act of printing or displaying those results.

output device A device used to present output, such as a monitor or a printer.

Paint A paint program that comes with Windows.

paint program An art program that keeps track of your image as a grid of dots.

pallet A set of numbered colors that the PC uses for an image.

palmtop PC A pocket-sized computer.

partition An area of a disk that Windows treats as a separate disk.

path The list of folders one goes through to get to a file.

PC (personal computer) A personal computer designed to run the Windows or DOS operating system.

PC Card A special expansion card type for laptops; also called PCMCIA.

PCI (Peripheral Component Interconnect) The most popular variety of local bus.

PCMCIA (Personal Computer Memory Card International Association) See **PC Card**.

Pentium A line of processors introduced by Intel in 1993 that can run Windows and both 16-bit and 32-bit programs. A Pentium processes information faster than earlier processors running at the same megahertz because of the Pentium's pipelining capability. The Pentium is available in models that run at speeds ranging from 60 to 300 megahertz.

Pentium II A line of processors introduced by Intel in 1997 that can run Windows and both 16-bit and 32-bit programs. A Pentium II processes information faster than the original Pentium running at the same speed because of improved pipelining. Additionally, most Pentium II models have a large built-in memory cache used to store information copied from RAM (random access memory) and access it more quickly than if it had to read the information from RAM each time it is needed. The Pentium II is currently available in models that run at speeds ranging from 233 to 400 megahertz.

Pentium III A line of processors introduced in 1999 by Intel that can run Windows and both 16-bit and 32-bit programs. The Pentium III has additional multimedia-oriented instructions that lets it process faster than a Pentium II running at the same speed. The Pentium III is currently available in various models running at speeds ranging from 450 to 550MHz.

peripheral Any device (such as a printer, speaker, or disk drive) added to or connected to the system unit.

Peripheral Component Interconnect See **PCI**.

personal computer A small computer system equipped with all the operating system, utility, and application software, and the input/output devices and other peripherals that an individual needs to perform computer operations.

photo enhancement program Software that enables you to alter and enhance scanned images.

photosensors Light detectors in a scanner.

pipelining A feature in the design of some processors that enables the processor to work on more than one command at a time.

PKZip A popular zip program.

point To move the pointer onto a specified screen item, as in *point to the My Computer icon*.

pointer A user-controlled onscreen item (usually an arrow) used to indicate other onscreen items.

port A connection point that governs and synchronizes the flow of data between the CPU and external devices, such as monitors, printers, and the mouse.

power supply A device in the system unit that converts power from the wall socket to the precise amounts that the PC needs.

presentation software A program that enables you to design onscreen or printed reports, demonstrations, and presentations.

printer An output device that transfers computer-generated words and images onto paper or other material.

processor A computer chip that performs calculations and comparisons on data.

program A series of instructions that the computer can execute to perform in a specific way. See *also* **software**.

program suite A group of programs (usually including a spreadsheet, a word processor, and a database) sold together that share information easily.

RAM (random access memory) A very quick form of storage that holds currently running programs and their data, sometimes referred to simply as memory.

random access memory See **RAM**.

ray tracing A form of modeling that creates realistic images by seeing how individual rays of light reflect and refract.

record A single entry in a database list.

Recycle Bin A place used to temporarily store deleted files.

regular RAM The old standard random access memory, which is slower than EDO RAM or SDRAM. *See also* **DRAM**.

removable hard disk A disk that holds large amounts of data and can be removed easily from the PC.

removable storage device A disk drive or tape drive used to store information on media that can be easily transferred to another PC.

resize Change the size of a window or other onscreen object.

resolution The number of dots that it takes to make up a digital image.

Restore button A title bar button that reduces the size of an open window.

right-click To quickly press and release the right mouse button.

sample A single slice of a sound lasting thousandths of a second, stored as a single number.

scanner A device that digitizes images from paper and stores the digitized information in files that can be read by a computer.

screen The monitor display.

screen saver A program that replaces the screen display with something interesting if you haven't used your keyboard or mouse for a set amount of time.

scrollable list A list in a dialog box that you can scroll through using up and down arrow buttons.

scrollbar A control bar on a window that enables you to select the portion of a larger document that you want to view.

SDRAM (synchronous dynamic random access memory) A very fast form of RAM.

select To choose a command from a menu, to indicate what item onscreen you want to work with (usually by clicking), or to highlight a block of text or other onscreen information in order to perform an operation on the highlighted material.

server A computer dedicated to storing files and sending them to other computers over a network.

shareware Programs that you can try for free. If you want to continue using them, you pay money to register them.

sheetfed scanner A scanner that moves paper, one sheet at a time, through the scanner.

Shift A key that you hold down while pressing other keys to get capital letters or other special characters and functions.

shortcut menu A context-sensitive menu that you get by right-clicking an onscreen item and that produces commands and options appropriate to that item.

SIMM (Single Inline Memory Module) One type of computer card that holds RAM (random access memory).

simulation A game or other program that enables you to simulate human involvement in a situation.

Single Inline Memory Module See **SIMM**.

slider A dialog box control that enables you to select a specific value by dragging an indicator between two end points.

software Computer programs, which are typically divided into two categories: operating systems (programs needed to operate the computer) and applications programs (programs used to perform tasks with the computer).

sound card An expansion card enables a personal computer to reproduce digitized sound. Also known as a soundboard.

speakers Devices that are used to project sound from your computer system.

spell check A word processing feature that checks your spelling.

spreadsheet A math program that creates a grid of rectangles into which you can put numbers, equations, or labels. The grid is also called a spreadsheet.

standby mode An energy-saving mode for your computer. In standby mode, your PC is effectively "asleep," with the hard disk and monitor turned off. You can quickly wake your PC out of standby mode by pressing the "on" button on the front of the PC.

startup disk A floppy disk with a simple operating system on it. A startup disk is used to start your system when there is a problem starting Windows from your hard drive.

storage The keeping of data.

submenu A menu that appears when you select a specific command from another menu.

SuperDisk A type of floppy drive that stores up to 120 megabytes on special disks. (Also called LS-120.)

surge A large increase in the amount of electricity coming from an electrical line.

surge protector A power socket extension that prevents surges from harming your PC.

synchronous dynamic random access memory See **SDRAM**.

system bus Circuitry on the motherboard that connects the CPU to other devices.

system unit The main box of your PC.

tab An item in a dialog box that enables you to pick a category of options and settings to display.

tape drive A storage device that can write a large amount of information to tape cartridges.

taskbar The bar on a Windows display that includes the Start button and buttons for the windows you currently have open.

terabyte About a trillion bytes.

text box A field in a dialog box into which you can type text.

thread A single discussion in a newsgroup.

title bar The bar at the very top of a window that contains the title of the active program or document and contains controls for the window display.

toner Black powder that a laser printer uses to create images on paper or other media.

toolbar A row of command buttons in a window.

tower PC A personal computer system unit designed to sit vertically.

unamplified speakers Speakers without a power adapter or batteries.

uniform resource locator *See* **URL**.

uninstalling Removing a piece of software from your hard disk.

upload Send a file from your PC to another computer via modem.

uploading program Software that handles uploading files.

URL (uniform resource locator) The Web address of a Web page or site.

Usenet The portion of the Internet that handles newsgroups.

utilities Programs that make your PC work faster, better, or easier.

video card An expansion card that handles all the information for the screen.

VLB (Video electronic standards association Local Bus) A no-longer-popular variety of local bus.

voice modem A modem that also enables you to use your PC as an answering machine.

Web *See* **WWW**.

Web browser A program that displays Web pages.

Web page A document on the World Wide Web.

Web server A computer that stores and transmits Web pages.

Web site An organized group of Web pages.

What's This? A button (marked with a ?) that provides context-sensitive help. To use the What's This? button, click it and then click the item for which you want help information.

window A rectangular area of the screen that a program uses to display information.

Windows A popular line of operating system software.

Windows 3.1 A pre-1995 version of Windows.

Windows 95 A major enhancement of Windows 3.1, released in 1995.

Windows 98 A minor enhancement of Windows 95, released in 1998.

Windows CE A special version of Windows for palmtop PCs and other devices.

Windows key A combination key with the Windows logo on it.

Windows NT A version of Windows for heavy-duty, networked, processing needs.

WinZip A popular zip program.

word processor A program that enables you to write, edit, and print text documents.

worksheet A spreadsheet grid.

World Wide Web *See* **WWW**.

write-protect switch A small tab on the back of a floppy disk, used to prevent the disk from accepting any changes or additions to the data that it contains.

WWW (World Wide Web) A huge system of connected documents spread across the Internet.

Xeon A line of advance processors designed for high-end business purposes. In 1999, Intel introduced Xeon versions of the Pentium II and Pentium III processors.

zip drive A type of floppy drive that stores up to 100 megabytes on special disks.

zip program A program that compresses several files into a single, smaller file (known as a zipped file) and is able to extract the compressed files back to their original state.

zipped file A file created by a zip program, storing several compressed files.

Index

files

Q-R

S

T

U

V

W

X-Z